W9-DEH-481

Fair Rate of Return in Property-Liability Insurance

Huebner International Series on Risk, Insurance, and Economic Security

Previously published books in the series:

Cummins, J. David; Smith, Barry D.; Vance, R. Neil; VanDerhei, Jack L.: *Risk Classification in Life Insurance*
Mintel, Judith: *Insurance Rate Litigation*
Cummins, J. David: *Strategic Planning and Modeling in Property-Liability Insurance*
Lemaire, Jean: *Automobile Insurance: Actuarial Models*
Rushing, William A.: *Social Functions and Economic Aspects of Health Insurance*

The objective of the series is to publish original research and advanced textbooks dealing with all major aspects of risk bearing and economic security. The emphasis is on books that will be of interest to an international audience. Interdisciplinary topics as well as those from traditional disciplines such as economics, risk and insurance, and actuarial science are within the scope of the series. The goal is to provide an outlet for imaginative approaches to problems in both the theory and practice of risk and economic security.

Fair Rate of Return in Property-Liability Insurance

edited by
J. David Cummins
Scott E. Harrington
Wharton School
University of Pennsylvania

Kluwer•Nijhoff Publishing
a member of the Kluwer Academic Publishers Group
Boston / Dordrecht / Lancaster

Distributors

for the United States and Canada: Kluwer Academic Publishers, 101 Philip Drive, Norwell, MA 02061, USA

for the UK and Ireland: Kluwer Academic Publishers, MTP Press Limited, Falcon House, Queen Square, Lancaster LA1 1RN, UK

for all other countries: Kluwer Academic Publishers Group, Distribution Centre, P. O. Box 322, 3300 AH Dordrecht, The Netherlands

Library of Congress Cataloging-in-Publication Data

Fair rate of return in property-liability insurance.
(Huebner international series on risk, insurance, and economic security)
Bibliography: p.
Includes index.
1. Insurance, Property—Rates and tables. 2. Insurance, Liability—Rates and tables. I. Cummins, J. David. II. Harrington, Scott E. III. Series.
HG8052.F35 1986 368'.09 86-10482
ISBN 0-89838-175-4

Printed in the United States.

Contents

Contributing Authors

Richard A. Cohn, Department of Finance, University of Hartford, West Hartford, CT, 06107.

J. David Cummins, Department of Insurance, Wharton School, University of Pennsylvania, Philadelphia, PA, 19104.

Richard A. Derrig, Massachusetts Rating Bureau, 40 Broad Street, Boston, MA, 02109.

William B. Fairley, Analysis and Inference, Inc., 10 Post Office Square, Suite 970, Boston, MA, 02109.

Scott E. Harrington, Department of Insurance, Wharton School, University of Pennsylvania, Philadelphia, PA, 19104.

Raymond D. Hill, Shearson-Lehman Brothers, American Express Plaza, 125 Broad Street, New York, NY, 10004.

Alan Kraus, Faculty of Commerce, University of British Columbia, 2053 Main Mall, Vancouver, British Columbia, Canada, V6T 1Y8.

Franco Modigliani, Sloan School of Management, Massachusetts Institute of Technology, Cambridge, MA, 02139.

Stewart C. Myers, Massachusetts Institute of Technology, 50 Memorial Drive, Cambridge, MA, 02139.

Stephen A. Ross, School of Organization and Management, Department of Economics, Yale University, 52 Hillhouse Avenue, New Haven, CT, 06520.

Andrew L. Turner, 3025 North Vassault, Tacoma, WA, 98407.

List of Tables and Figures

Tables

Figure

Preface

Property-liability insurance rates for most lines of business are regulated in about one-half of the states. In most cases, this means that rates must be filed with the state insurance commissioner and approved prior to use. The remainder of the states have various forms of competitive rating laws. These either require that rates be filed prior to use but need not be approved or that rates need not be filed at all. State rating laws are summarized in Rand Corporation (1985).

The predominant form of insurance rate regulation, prior approval, began in the late 1940s following the U.S. Supreme Court decision in *United States* vs. *South-Eastern Underwriters Association*, 322 U.S. 533 (1944). This was an antitrust case involving one of four regional associations of insurance companies, which constituted an insurance cartel. The case struck down an earlier decision, *Paul* vs. *Virginia*, 8 Wall 168 (1869), holding that the business of insurance was not interstate commerce and hence that state regulation of insurance did not violate the commerce clause of the U.S. Constitution. Following *South-Eastern Underwriters*, the United States Congress passed the McCarran-Ferguson Act, which held that continued state regulation and taxation of insurance was in the public interest. The act also held that the federal antitrust laws would not apply to insurance to the extent that the business was adequately regulated by state law. (See U.S. Department of Justice 1977.)

The states and the insurance industry reacted to McCarran-Ferguson by drafting and passing laws known as the All-Industry bills. The bills were the result of a compromise between the insurance industry and the state insurance commissioners. Most states had adopted the All-Industry bills by the late 1940s.

The principal thrust of the All-Industry bills was to control the rating bureaus, which had been a driving force behind the cartel, through prior approval rate regulation. Essentially the bills legalized ratemaking in concert (i.e., through bureaus) using the traditional credibility rationale but put in place a regulatory system designed to prevent the bureaus from misusing their power (see Crane 1972).

Although California adopted a competitive rating law in 1947, regulated rates were prevalent in the rest of the country until the late 1960s. During the 1960s several factors combined to motivate a reevaluation of rate regulation. (1) The so-called direct writing insurance companies, such as State Farm and Allstate, had grown rapidly during the 1950s and early 1960s by using superior technology (i.e., their own agents rather than the traditional independent agency system). Their efficiency advantage and large volume enabled the direct writers to price independently of the bureaus and below bureau rates. In addition, rate deviations by bureau firms became easier to obtain and somewhat more widespread. (2) The growth in the number of automobiles removed much of the credibility rationale for joint data collection and pricing in automobile insurance. And (3) the increase in inflation and the accompanying rise in interest rates led to increasing pressure on insurers to recognize the investment income earned on policyholder funds in their ratemaking formulas.

The states responded to these pressures in two major ways: Some states (e.g., Florida) deregulated property-liability insurance rates, based on the hypothesis that insurance markets were competitive and hence that competitive forces would drive prices and profits to the appropriate level. A few states (e.g., Texas and New Jersey) elected to retain rate regulation but to require insurers to recognize investment income in ratemaking. These states essentially were seeking to ensure that insurers would earn neither more nor less than the fair rate of return for risk bearing.

Even though the fair rate of return issue was introduced in the context of rate regulation, it is also important in a deregulated environment. This is the case because regulators should monitor insurance markets under deregulation to ensure that prices and profits are competitive—e.g., that insurers are not earning monopoly rents. The purpose of this book is to present the best research that has been conducted on the fair rate of return issue in property-liability insurance.

In the spirit of the *Hope Natural Gas* decision, fair rate of return analysis in property-liability insurance has attempted to determine the rate of return "commensurate with the returns on investment in other enterprises having corresponding risks" (320 U.S. 591 (1944)). Two principal approaches have been taken: (1) book value methods and (2) market value methods.

The initial fair rate of return studies in insurance adopted the book value approach. These studies looked at accounting returns in insurance (usually, rate of return on equity or on total assets) and compared them to returns in other industries. The variance of the book rate of return was adopted as the appropriate measure of risk. Insurance generally was found to earn a lower book rate of return than other industries with comparable variance of return. (See, for example, Arthur D. Little 1967; and Forbes 1971.) More recent studies (National Association of Insurance Commissioners 1983; and Williams 1983) also have used book return comparisons and reached similar conclusions. A critical analysis of the book value method utilized in New Jersey is presented in Cummins and Chang (1983).

There are two major problems with book return comparisons that severely limit their relevance in determining the fair rate of return. First, insurers are financial institutions, and a very high proportion of their assets represent marketable securities. Nevertheless, the book return methods compare insurers to many other industries in the economy (e.g., manufacturing) whose assets are valued at depreciated book value rather than by any method approaching true market value. The wide divergence in valuation techniques across industries renders book return comparisons virtually meaningless. Second, the adoption of the variance of book returns as the relevant measure of risk is totally without theoretical foundation. Indeed, a regression equation fitted to the book return—variance of return data in National Association of Insurance Commissioners (1983) has a negative slope (see Venezian 1984). That is, if one adopts book measures as relevant, industries with higher variance should earn lower returns. In the absence of any theoretical or conceptual foundation, the comparison of book returns and variances across industries is of no real value in determining the fair rate of return.

The other major method for determining fair rate of return is modern financial theory. This is the method reflected in the papers published in this book. Modern financial theory was first proposed for use in property-liability ratemaking by Cooper (1974) and Biger and Kahane (1978). Many of the influential papers were prepared in connection with automobile insurance rate hearings in Massachusetts, which has been the leading state in the use of modern financial theory in insurance rate regulation. The regulatory experience in Massachusetts is discussed in chapter 6 of this book by Richard A. Derrig.

The initial application of modern financial theory in ratemaking was based on work by William Fairley. The initial paper developing the Fairley methodology (Fairley 1979) is reprinted as chapter 1 of this book. An important extension of the Fairley methodology, by Raymond Hill and

Franco Modigliani, is presented as chapter 2.

One of the salient characteristics of the work by Biger and Kahane, Fairley, and Hill and Modigliani is that the investable funds generated due to the delay between premium collection and the payment of claims is modeled by a single factor (often called the funds-generating factor). The role of this factor is to incorporate into the models an approximation of a discounted cash flow approach. (The approximation can lead to errors unless some very strict conditions are met. See Cummins and Chang 1983.) Currently, rate regulation in Massachusetts utilizes an explicit discounted cash flow approach rather than the funds-generating factor that was used originally. The discounted cash flow methodology is based on work by Stewart Myers and Richard Cohn, which is published as chapter 3 of this book.

Finally, the book contains two theoretical chapters that extend the frontiers of fair rate of return analysis in insurance. Chapter 4, by Andrew Turner, incorporates insurance into a two-period capital asset pricing framework. This chapter is important because it shows that individual insurable risk is significant in asset pricing even if this risk is nonsystematic. This is contrary to the usual contentions of capital market theorists that a significant proportion of insurance risk "averages out" and hence is not compensated in market prices. The work by Alan Kraus and Stephen Ross (1982) is reprinted as chapter 5. This study, bases fair rate of return on arbitrage pricing theory rather than the Sharpe-Lintner capital asset pricing model that underlies the work in chapters 1 through 4. Their chapter considers the impact of inflation and models the claims runoff process using an exponential hypothesis.

Overall, the chapters in this book represent the state of the art of fair rate of return regulation in insurance. Along with a handful of recent journal articles (e.g., Cummins and Harrington 1985) they form the essential body of knowledge that will provide the underpinnings for all future work in this field.

References

Arthur D. Little, Inc. 1967. *Prices and Profits in the Property and Liability Insurance: A Report to the Amercian Insurance Association*. Boston: Arthur D. Little.

Biger, Nahum, and Yehuda Kahane. 1978. Risk considerations in insurance rate making. *Journal of Risk and Insurance* 45:121–132.

Cooper, Robert W. 1974. *Investment Return and Property-Liability Insurance Ratemaking*. Homewood, IL: Richard D. Irwin.

Crane, Frederick G. 1972. Insurance rate regulation: The reasons why. *Journal of Risk and Insurance* 39:511–534.

Cummins, J. David, and Scott E. Harrington. 1985. Property-liability insurance rate regulation: Estimation of underwriting betas using quarterly profit data. *Journal of Risk and Insurance* 52:16–43.

Cummins, J. David, and Lena Chang. 1983. An analysis of the New Jersey formula for including investment income in property-liability insurance ratemaking. *Journal of Insurance Regulation* 1:555–573.

Fairley, William. 1979. Investment income and profit margins in property-liability insurance: Theory and empirical results. *Bell Journal of Economics* 10:192–210.

Forbes, Stephen W. 1971. Rates of return in the nonlife insurance industry. *Journal of Risk and Insurance* 38:409–422.

Harrington, Scott E. 1984. The impact of rate regulation on prices and underwriting results in the property-liability industry: A survey. *Journal of Risk and Insurance* 51 (December):577–623.

Kraus, Alan and Stephen A. Ross. 1982. The determinants of fair profits for the property-liability insurance firm. *Journal of Finance* 37 (September):1015–1028.

Mintel, Judith. 1983. *Insurance Rate Litigation*. Hingham, MA: Kluwer-Nijhoff.

National Association of Insurance Commissioners. 1983. *Report of the Advisory Committee To the NAIC Task Force on Profitability and Investment Income*. Kansas City, MO: The Association.

Rand Corporation. 1985. *Automobile Accident Compensation. IV: State Rules*. Santa Monica, CA.: Rand Corporation.

U.S. Department of Justice. 1977. *The Pricing and Marketing of Insurance*. Stock No. 027-000-00477-6. Washington, D.C.: U.S. Government Printing Office.

Venezian, Emilio C. 1984. Are insurers underearning? *Journal of Risk and Insurance* 51:150–156.

Williams, C. Arthur, Jr. 1983. Regulating property and liability insurance rates through excess profits statutes. *Journal of Risk and Insurance* 50:445–472.

Fair Rate of Return in Property-Liability Insurance

1 INVESTMENT INCOME AND PROFIT MARGINS IN PROPERTY-LIABILITY INSURANCE: THEORY AND EMPIRICAL RESULTS

William B. Fairley

Introduction

The present analysis applies the capital-asset pricing model (CAPM) of contemporary financial theory to derive risk-adjusted rates of return that the capital markets require of stock property-liability insurers. The required profit margins in insurance premiums for the major property-

---

The point of departure of the work reported here was the May 1975 decision on workers' compensation rates by the Massachusetts Commissioner of Insurance, James M. Stone, who has also contributed very usefully to the entire effort. The chapter draws on testimony of the Massachusetts State Rating Bureau presented at rate hearings in the Division of Insurance. The views in it, however, are the author's and do not necessarily represent the position of the Massachusetts Division of Insurance, where the author was formerly a staff member. I am grateful, for comments on an earlier version, to Carliss Baldwin, Fisher Black, Lena Chang, Andrew F. Giffen, Raymond D. Hill, James H. Hunt, Peter R. Jones, Paul L. Joskow, Richard O. Michaud, Stefan Peters, and an anonymous referee. For stimulating hearing examination I thank attorneys Acheson H. Callaghan, Jr., Steward W. Kemp, and Michael B. Meyer. None of these helpful people is responsible for the views expressed or for any errors.

Editor's Note: A number of minor editorial changes in the original version of this paper were made by the editor.

liability lines that are consistent with these rates of return are derived using estimated multiquarter cash flows for premiums and costs. These margins have been used by the Massachusetts Commissioner of Insurance in rate decisions or rate reviews for all the major property-liability lines and for medical malpractice insurance. They represent an effort to bring the consideration of insurer profits within a framework of modern financial theory. A distinctive feature of the margins developed here is that, because they do not depend upon actual investment results for insurers' portfolios, they offer a nonintrusive regulatory solution of the long controversy over the use of investment income in insurance rate setting.[1]

In almost every state today property-liability insurance rate filings contain traditional profit factors adopted at various times in the past by the National Association of Insurance Commissioners.[2] For example, in auto they are generally 5 percent of premiums, in homeowners 6 percent, and in workers' compensation 2.5 percent. No explicit risk-return theory was used to justify these figures, and they are now widely acknowledged to be essentially unsupported. The United States Supreme Court in the *Hope Natural Gas* case (*Hope*), in which it set out the still-reigning legal standard for judging the reasonableness of rates of return in regulated industries, referred to returns "commensurate with returns on investments in other enterprises having corresponding risks" but it did not define "risk" operationally or indicate an explicit theory of the required returns to that risk.[3]

Some theory of risk-adjusted equilibrium rates of return appears to be needed to make normative sense out of regulated rates of return and profit margins that are consistent with them.[4] In what sense do investors require certain rates of return; and, in particular, what do they require in the way of compensation for "risk"? It is a fair question to ask whether the CAPM, although widely recognized as one of the central paradigms of financial theory, is sufficiently strong to be relied upon as a basis for estimating required rates of return. Testimony of witnesses in the field of finance at hearings in the Massachusetts Insurance Department has consistently favored or been sympathetic to the department's effort to apply the CAPM in rate regulation.[5] Other experts in finance, such as Bicksler (1976) and Robichek (1978), have supported the use of the CAPM. However, attack on the usefulness of the model in some rate proceedings has occurred. (See, for example, the testimony of Brigham (1977) at hearings of the Oregon Public Utilities Commission, which utilizes the CAPM in rate-of-return determinations.)

A complete answer to the question of adequacy of the CAPM for use in rate regulation would require a lengthy discussion, not given here, of the role of models in administrative proceedings. The interested reader is referred to a very useful discussion of key issues in Finkelstein (1973). In the context of actual decision making, a trite but sometimes overlooked point is that choices must be made. The option of reserving judgment until more evidence comes in is usually not available. It follows that the questions of "adequacy" cannot be answered for a single proposal considered in isolation, but only in relation to the alternatives. It is also of interest to note that the Supreme Judicial Court of Massachusetts, the state's highest court, in upholding the Insurance Commissioner's decision on 1976 auto rates, relied on target returns in auto insurance determined from the CAPM.[6]

Simplifying Assumptions in Use of the CAPM

Application of the CAPM rests on simplifying assumptions with regard to multiperiod valuation of equity and the treatment of the solvency of companies. Fama (1977) and Myers and Turnbull (1977) consider the application of single-period CAPM models to real-world multiperiod problems. Myers and Turnbull tentatively conclude, subject to "a long list of simplifying assumptions," that "no serious errors are introduced by discounting cash-flow streams at one-period expected rates of return inferred from observed betas." Fama is likewise cautious, but he states that it might be reasonable to make assumptions that justify the use of a "single risk-adjusted discount rate or cost of capital that can be applied to all cash flows." While theoretical work in this area continues, it seems reasonable to apply single discount rates based upon estimated betas, as is done below.

The probability of insolvency is not considered within the simple CAPM framework used in the present analysis. Insolvency risk has been discussed in an exploratory way by Hill (1978) and Munch and Smallwood (1978). It is clear that the proper treatment of insolvency risk in the context of the CAPM is extremely difficult and not yet well advanced. To the consumer, insolvency has the potential cost of nonpayment of "debt," although in practice, state guaranty funds almost always protect the individual policyholder from nonpayment of claims. The actual dollar volume of insolvencies has been tiny in comparison with total premiums, and in most cases the insolvencies have resulted from incompetence or fraud and not from typical sources of variability in investment or underwriting results.

Though state regulations and industry practice have sufficed in the past to hold insolvencies to a minimal level, there is no guarantee within the existing structure of the market that changed circumstances would not threaten that record. In particular, companies can increase or decrease the riskiness of their books of business without effective regulatory control—an illustration of which is apparently given by the widely publicized problems of the Government Employees Insurance Company (GEICO). Increasing riskiness threatens the stability of companies and, in some instances, service to consumers, while decreasing riskiness is most often accomplished by restricting the availability of insurance. How important these outcomes are for consumer welfare depends greatly on the details of each state's insurance statutes.[7] From the point of view of determining insurance rates, however, no case has been made that these considerations call for higher or for lower profit margins in the rates. Thus, while further attention to the probability of insolvency and its eventual inclusion within broader models is merited, there is at present no compelling reason to reject the application of the CAPM in rate regulation because a complete treatment of insolvency is not at hand.

Regulatory Use of Profit Margins

What regulatory use, if any, should be made of the profit margins derived here? This is a question that is distinct from that of the validity and accuracy of the margins themselves. The answer depends upon the form of rate regulation—including no regulation at all—in a state. No "market failures" argument for any particular form of regulation is made here. Rather, the point of view adopted is that so long as profit margin allowances are used by state—and, possibly in the future, by federal—regulators in any form, they should be based upon the best available theory and evidence. The margins derived below are advanced as meeting that criterion. In states with "open competition" rating laws, where the role of the state regulator is only to monitor the effectiveness of competition, the present margins should be of interest as one part of the analysis that is essential to informed monitoring. In states with some kind of prior-approval rating law, the present margins are proposed as substitutes for the traditional factors.

The Literature

Jensen (1972) discusses the origins of the CAPM in the Markowitz theory of portfolio selection and provides an exposition and review. Ross (1978) gives a more recent discussion of the theory and its competitors. The model has been introduced in regulatory proceedings in other industries. See for example, references to and discussion of public utility applications in Myers (1972a, b), Peseau and Zepp (1978), and Pettway (1978). Quirin and Waters (1975), Massachusetts Division of Insurance (1976a, b), Hill (1978), and Munch and Smallwood (1978), among others, have applied the CAPM to returns of property-liability insurers. Financial models for returns developed by Quirin and Waters and by Hill are for an assumed case in which premiums are received at the beginning of a period and claims are all paid at the end. Quirin and Waters assume underwriting has a zero systematic risk and deduce that in this event the underwriting profit margin should be the negative of the risk-free return. Hill, and Munch and Smallwood, permit nonzero systematic risk of underwriting and derive for the single-period model a solution for underwriting profit that equals the negative of the risk-free return plus a term that compensates for underwriting risk. These analytical results are consistent with those derived below. The analysis in the present paper, which was developed for application in rate filings (see Massachusetts Division of Insurance, 1976a,b and 1977) differs in permitting cash flows in any pattern over several years and, using measurements of quarterly cash flows, in determining profit margins explicitly by line of insurance for the major property-liability lines.

The second section of this chapter develops a financial model of an insurer that describes the sources of its returns. The third section determines risk-adjusted target returns for insurers based upon the CAPM. The fourth section derives analytical solutions for underwriting profit margins that are consistent with the target returns derived, and the fifth section makes estimates of systematic risks and couples these with estimated multiquarter cash flows to give estimates of required profit margins by line. The sixth and final section discusses implications of adopting these margins in place of the traditional factors wherever they are called for in rate filings.

A Financial Model for Returns

This section develops a financial model for returns, actual or anticipated, of a property-liability insurer operating in a competitive market. The basic outline of the model is standard (see, for example, Joskow 1973, pp. 412–413).

Earnings and Return on Equity

For simplicity, consider first a single insurer starting out to sell or "write" insurance in only one line and paying no taxes. Suppose it writes expected premiums in the amount $\bar{M}$ for a given policy year of coverage and begins the year with a market value of equity equal to V_E. The premium-to-capital ratio, $\bar{M}/V_E$, will be of interest and is denoted s.

The typical cash-flow pattern in the business is early receipt of premiums followed by payment of claims and expenses in subsequent months or years. This early positive net cash flow is invested at an average annual return of $\bar{r}_A$ expected as of the beginning of the policy year. Barred quantities will in general denote conditional expected values of random variables as of the beginning of the policy year.[8]

The market value of the investment earnings expected as of the beginning of the policy year from the cash-flow pattern is some multiple, k, of $\bar{r}_A$ and of $\bar{M}$, or $\bar{r}_A k\bar{M}$ in total. The longer the cash flow, that is, the longer the average time between receipt of premiums and payout in claims and expenses, the larger the value of k. Earnings $\bar{r}_A k\bar{M}$ can also be interpreted as expected earnings for one year on a virtual asset of size $k\bar{M}$ at yield $\bar{r}_A$. In a steady-state model in which premiums $\bar{M}$ are written annually, the cash flow would, in fact, create such an asset over time. The constant k can therefore be interpreted as the average amount of investable funds created by the cash flow per dollar of annual premium.

An insurer also expects to earn the return $\bar{r}_A V_E$ from investment of equity at yield $\bar{r}_A$. No distinction is introduced here between the market value of equity, V_E, and various accounting or book values of equity. The two may of course diverge over time, but in competitive markets the expected book and market values of new equity capital put into the insurance business should be the same. Since the *Hope* standard is a capital-attraction standard, it is appropriate in the analysis of returns and of target returns to treat V_E as if it were new equity.[9]

Besides investment returns from cash flow or equity, the profit margin on sales—what is customarily called the "underwriting margin"—which may be positive or negative, is a source of earnings for insurers. Denote the expected profit margin $\bar{p}$, so that total expected earnings on sales is $\bar{p}\bar{M}$.

Total expected market-valued earnings to be realized at the end of the policy year are then $\bar{r}_A(k\bar{M} + V_E) + \bar{p}\bar{M}$. Dividing this total by the value of equity gives the expected return on equity, $\bar{r}_E$:

$$\bar{r}_E = [\bar{r}_A(k\bar{M} + V_E) + \bar{p}\bar{M}]/V_E \tag{1.1}$$

Substituting s for $\bar{M}/V_E$ gives

$$\bar{r}_E = \bar{r}_A(ks + 1) + \bar{p}s \tag{1.1a}$$

An appendix, which is available from the author, may be referred to for a more detailed accounting of the earnings sources.

Table 1-1. Returns on Cash Flow and Average Reserves Per Dollar of Premiums by Line of Insurance

Line of Insurance	*Return on Cash Flow*[a]	*Average Reserves Per Dollar of Premiums* (k_n)	*Total U.S. 1975 Earned Premiums*[b] (*$ billion*)
Auto bodily injury	16.8%	1.60	4.8
Auto property damage	3.2	0.31	7.7
Homeowners	3.7	0.35	3.4
Workers' compensation	16.8	1.60	4.6
Weighted average	9.5	0.91	20.5
Medical malpractice	40.3	3.74	—

Sources: (a) Massachusetts Division of Insurance (1978). Assumes average discount rate, $\bar{r}_A$, of 10.5 percent. (b) Best (1976) adjusted to Massachusetts categories.

Figure 1-1. Cumulative Cash Flow
(proportion of premium dollar available for investment)

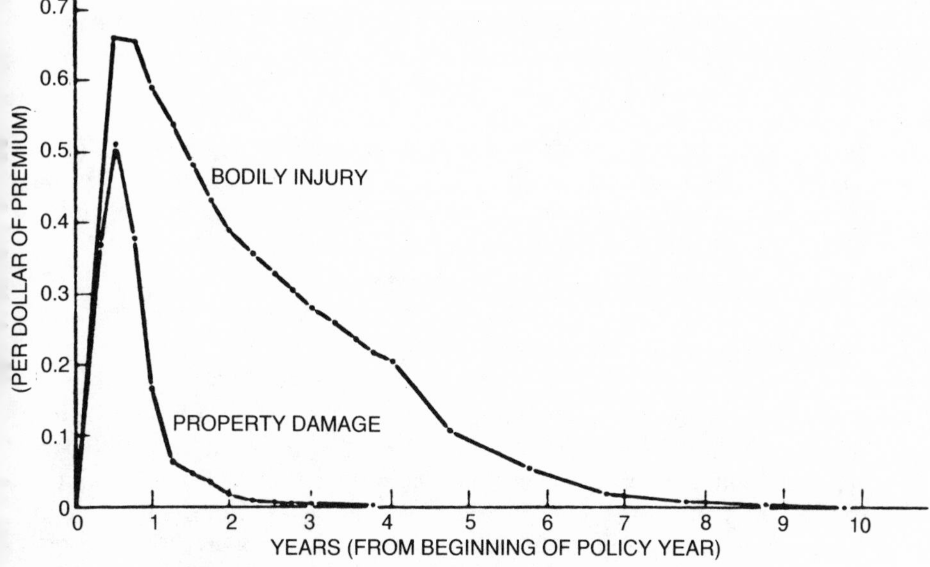

Source: Massachusetts Division of Insurance (1978).

If an insurer writes a mix of lines with investable funds per dollar of premiums k_N for line N, then k in equation (1.1a) is interpreted as an average of the k_N's, weighted by the proportions of premiums written in the lines. Similarly, the profit margin $\bar{p}$ may be interpreted as a weighted average of profit margins by line, the $\bar{p}_N$'s.

Estimated values of k_N for the major lines and for medical malpractice are given in table 1-1. Figure 1-1 plots the cumulative cash flows over time for auto bodily injury and for auto property-damage coverages and shows the dramatic differences that exist between the lines in the lengths of these flows.[10]

Underwriting Profit and the Return on Liabilities

The investable funds $k\bar{M}$ are generated by policyholders' premiums. At the same time they represent liabilities for future payments of claims and expenses. From this point of view, since total assets of V_A equal $k\bar{M} + V_E$, $k\bar{M}$ is the value of liabilities, V_L. By using perfect economic or market-value accounting, as opposed to book accounting, then for a hypothetical market-value balance sheet evaluated as of the beginning of the policy year, the market value of the firm, V_E, equals $V_A - V_L$. It follows that $\bar{r}_E V_E$ must equal $\bar{r}_A V_A - \bar{r}_L V_L$, where $\bar{r}_L$ is the expected return paid on liabilities. From (1.1a) we see that the expected underwriting margin can be factored as follows:

$$\bar{p} = -\bar{r}_L k \tag{1.2}$$

If the expected return paid on liabilities is positive, then equation (1.2) shows that the expected underwriting margin of insurers is negative in a competitive market. Underwriting would have a positive margin only if the return on liabilities were negative.

Target Returns

An insurer combines earnings on a product sales margin or underwriting profits with investment earnings on a portfolio created by policyholder-supplied funds and on its own capital. The systematic risk, like its earnings, can be analyzed as the sum of risks from the underwriting function and from the investment-return function. This additive property follows from the linearity of the covariance operator in the definition of beta.

Definitions of Betas

Under the CAPM, an insurer's risk-adjusted after-tax target return, r_E^g, is given by the sum of the yield on a risk-free security, $\bar{r}_f$, and a risk premium equal to the beta coefficient, β_E—the measure of systematic risk of the insurer—times the average market risk premium, $\bar{r}_m - \bar{r}_f$—where $\bar{r}_m$ is the expected return on an overall market index:

$$r_E^g = \bar{r}_f + \beta_E(\bar{r}_m - \bar{r}_f) \tag{1.3}$$

The beta coefficient, β_E, is by definition:

$$\beta_E = \text{cov}(r_E, r_m)/\text{var}(r_m) \tag{1.4}$$

Quantities without bars refer to the random variables whose expected values are the corresponding barred quantities.

To analyze the overall beta, β_E, in terms of the systematic risks associated with the investment and the underwriting sides of the business, betas of asset and liability returns are defined. The beta coefficient for returns on assets, β_A, is $\text{cov}(r_A, r_M)/\text{var}(r_m)$, and the beta coefficient, β_L, for returns on liabilities is $\text{cov}(r_L, r_m)/\text{var}(r_m)$. Since the profit margin p equals $-kr_L$, from the random variable analogue of equation (1.2), a beta coefficient, β_p, for profits can be defined as[11]

$$\beta_p = -k\beta_L \tag{1.5}$$

Systematic Risk of Insurers Analyzed

Investment and underwriting components of the systematic risk of insurers can now be distinguished by taking covariances of both sides of (1.1a), modified by the substitution of random variables for expected values, and dividing through by $\text{var}(r_m)$ to obtain an expression for the beta of equity in terms of the betas of investments and of underwriting:

$$\beta_E = \beta_A(ks + 1) + \beta_p s \tag{1.6}$$

For a particular line N, substitute $\beta_{E,N}$, k_N, and $\beta_{p,N}$ for β_E, k, and β_p, respectively. Such an accounting for the components of systematic risk follows suggestions made by Black (1975) in testimony at Massachusetts hearings on 1976 auto insurance rates.

Beta coefficients, such as β_E, are usually defined only for overall returns on equity. But, given a linear equation in the returns and linearity of the covariance operator, equation (1.6) gives an analysis of β_E in terms of an investment component, $\beta_A(ks + 1)$, and an underwriting component, $\beta_p s$. The underwriting component of the systematic risk of property-liability insurers, based on estimates of the parameters in (1.6), is for all lines combined, only about one-fifth of the total systematic risk. The investment component is about four-fifths. Thus, although very substantial fluctuations are characteristic of underwriting profits, there is no evidence that the market regards these swings as cause for much additional return over and above the returns it expects for the systematic risk of investments.

Systematic Risk of Underwriting by Line

To determine profit margins by line it is essential to estimate the systematic risk of underwriting by line of insurance. Unfortunately, actual companies are multiline, and direct determination of market betas is not possible. Use of accounting data by line leads to biased estimates of market betas (Hill 1978). It is possible that indirect regression estimates will be useful.[12] Until better estimates are available, expression (1.5) can be utilized to determine by-line estimates of beta, $\beta_{p,N}$. Substituting in (1.5) the by-line size of liabilities per dollar of premium, k_N, for the average value of k and assuming that β_L is constant by line yields

$$\beta_{p,N} = -k_N \beta_L \tag{1.7}$$

Expression (1.7) breaks the systematic risk per dollar of profits by line into a dependence on the size of liabilities per dollar of premiums by line, k_N, and on the systematic risk per dollar of liabilities, β_L. The values of k_N vary greatly. For example, the ratio between the liabilities generated by medical malpractice premiums and by auto property-damage premiums is over ten to one. In the insurance industry, where "risk" is generally conceived of in terms of total variability, the lines with the longer cash flows are viewed as the "riskiest." It is of interest to note in passing therefore that $\beta_{p,N}$, the measure of systematic risk by line given by equation (1.7), also increases directly with the length of the cash flow—a property that accords with industry views about risk.

The assumption in equation (1.7) that β_L is constant by line is important and strong, and future work should be directed at relaxing it. However, as will now be argued, expression (1.7) for systematic risk by line probably does capture the main effect by line, it contains no known biases, and the errors made in using it are not demonstrably more serious than in using any other.

Liabilities of most lines would appear to be largely independent of overall market movements, since neither the contingent events that provide opportunities to file claims nor the propensity to file claims given such events would seem to be much affected by market movements. There are therefore no strong a priori or theoretical grounds for supposing either that β_L is very large or that it would vary much between lines. The assumption that β_L is zero has been made by some (Quirin and Waters 1975). The estimates that have been made of β_L, as an average over all lines, are small, as shown in the next section; and these results are at least consistent with the prior expectation that for most lines β_L is small. It should be kept in mind that small systematic risk by line is consistent with the known presence of substantial variability in the underwriting profit margins of property-liability insurers. Under the CAPM it is only the nondiversifiable component of that variability that is relevant to market equilibrium returns on securities.

If individual values of β_L by line are small in absolute terms then, even if ratios between them are large, the numerical solutions for profit margins derived below will not be very sensitive to an assumption that β_L is the same for all lines. If it turned out that a small average value of β_L masked the existence of individual values of β_L by line that were of opposite sign but substantial in absolute value, then profit factors computed on the assumption of constant β_L would be in error. Of course, there is no reason to believe that the traditional profit factors are more correct in their pattern by line. On balance it seems reasonable at the present time to adopt the assumption of a common value of β_L for all lines for which there is no a priori reason to worry about a deviation. Credit insurance might be one such exception, but the major lines discussed below are not.

Analytical Profit Solutions

The required or target profit margin by line, consistent with the *Hope* standard, as that is interpreted through the CAPM, is the value $\bar{p}_N$ that equilibrates total expected return, $\bar{r}_{E,N}$, and target return, $r^g_{E,N}$. It is the solution for $\bar{p}_N$ of the equation

$$r^g_{E,N} = \bar{r}_{E,N} \tag{1.8}$$

The solution is obtained by substituting the market-equilibrium value for $\bar{r}_A$, $\bar{r}_f + \beta_A(\bar{r}_m - \bar{r}_f)$, and k_N for k in (1.1a) to determine $\bar{r}_{E,N}$ as

$$\bar{r}_{\mathrm{E,N}} = [\bar{r}_f + \beta_A(\bar{r}_m - \bar{r}_f)](k_N s + 1) + \bar{p}_N s \tag{1.9}$$

Substituting for β_E its breakdown in terms of β_A and β_p given by equation

(1.6), and k_N for k into equation (1.3), determines $r^g_{E,N}$ as

$$r^g_{E,N} = \bar{r}_f + [\beta_A(k_N s + 1) + \beta_{p,N} s](\bar{r}_m - \bar{r}_f) \tag{1.10}$$

Setting (1.9) equal to (1.10) and solving for $\bar{p}_N$, the terms involving the systematic risk of investments cancel, as do all terms depending on the premium-to-capital ratio s, and the solution is

$$\bar{p}_N = -k_N\bar{r}_f + \beta_{p,N}(\bar{r}_m - \bar{r}_f) \tag{1.11}$$

Substituting $-k_N\beta_L$ for $\beta_{p,N}$ in (1.11) shows $\bar{p}_N$ to equal $-k_N\bar{r}_L$, since the return $\bar{r}_L$ is equal to $\bar{r}_f + \beta_L(\bar{r}_m - \bar{r}_f)$. This result for $\bar{p}_N$ is consistent with expression (1.2).

Properties of Required Profit Margins

An implicit interest payment to insureds for the "loan" of their cash flow appears as the first summand, $-k_N\bar{r}_f$, in the solution (1.11) for $\bar{p}_N$. It reduces required profits directly with the size, k_N, of the loan and the prevailing rate of interest on risk-free securities, $\bar{r}_f$. A risk premium for the systematic risks of underwriting is given by the second summand in equation (1.11), $\beta_{p,N}(\bar{r}_m - \bar{r}_f)$, which by (1.7) also equals $-k_N\beta_L(\bar{r}_m - \bar{r}_f)$. If β_L is negative, as estimates shown below indicate, this risk premium also raises required profits directly with the size of the loan. However, the empirical results also indicate that, in terms of the dependence of the solution $\bar{p}_N$ on k_N, the first summand in equation (1.11) dominates the second in absolute value so that the required profit margins do vary inversely with the size of the loan.

The profit-margin solutions of equation (1.11) do not depend upon the composition or the actual outcomes of investment portfolios of individual companies. They depend only on the government-bond yield, the lengths of the cash flows of each line, and the systematic risk of underwriting. These quantities are assumed here to be either the same for all companies or are established at average industry values—a procedure that is discussed below. Consequently, under these assumptions no direct regulation, or even measurement, of actual investment income of individual companies is required in using these margins as profit factors in rate filings—a feature that is an attractive aspect of the new margins.

Companies with riskier strategies have higher anticipated returns, but they are also required to compensate investors at higher rates for bearing greater risks. Thus, while their anticipated returns are greater than for less venturesome companies, the target returns are also commensurately higher. As a result, the solutions $\bar{p}_N$ are independent of $\bar{r}_A$. Shareholders of companies with the riskier investment portfolios will require—and in the long run can expect to receive—greater returns than shareholders of other companies. Policyholders of stock companies, who do not share in the investment risks, pay exactly the same premiums for their insurance regardless of their company's investment policies. Policyholders who seek to participate in the variable investment results of company portfolios can buy shares of stock insurers or, alternatively, buy insurance from mutual companies.

Fractional Investment Shares

In principle, a company could operate as a mixed stock-mutual company by permitting shareholders to share in only a specified fraction of the investment returns from policyholders' funds. Suppose this fraction were x, so that shareholders would expect to earn $x\bar{r}_A ks$ on policyholders' funds. Then the solution of equation (1.8), with the term $x\bar{r}_A ks$ in place of $\bar{r}_A ks$, for $\bar{p}_N(x)$ is

$$\bar{p}_N(x) = -xk_N\bar{r}_f + \beta_{p,N}(\bar{r}_m - \bar{r}_f) \tag{1.12}$$

If x is 1, then $p_N(1)$ is the same as (1.11); if x is 0, then $\bar{p}_N(0)$ equals $\beta_{p,N}(\bar{r}_m - \bar{r}_f)$, and the shareholders receive a larger underwriting profit margin than is given by (1.11). When shareholders take all of the investment returns, the company can offer a lower underwriting margin and therefore a lower premium for insurance, and shareholders shoulder both the risk and the return of investing policyholders' funds. When policyholders take all the investment returns, they pay an initially higher profit margin and thus a higher premium, but they receive the variable dividends that are based upon investment results. This is the position of mutual insurance.

The procedure adopted by some states, such as New Jersey, for including investment income in ratemaking has the property of fractional investment sharing just described. In the New Jersey formula, current investment income, as distinguished from capital gains, is subtracted from a customary base-allowance yield to determine the profit allowance. A substantial part of investment risk is still retained by shareholders, however, since capital gains are excluded.[13]

Taxes and Interfirm Differences

The introduction of corporate income taxes modifies the solution (1.11) for $\bar{p}_N$ by adding to it a term depending upon the tax rate, t, and the premium-to-capital ratio, s: that is, $\bar{r}_f t/[(1 - t)s]$. The new expression for $\bar{p}_N$ is derived by substituting after-tax expected returns, $(1 - t)\bar{r}_{E,N}$, for $\bar{r}_{E,N}$ in equation (1.9) and after-tax beta, $(1 - t)\beta_E$, for β_E in equation (1.6):

$$\bar{p}_N = -k_N\bar{r}_f + \beta_{p,N}(\bar{r}_m - \bar{r}_f) + \bar{r}_f t/[(1 - t)s] \tag{1.11a}$$

This simplified analysis of taxes abstracts from complexities of detail such as the differing tax treatments of the different types of securities and of capital gains versus dividend or interest income and from carry-forward or carry-back of underwriting losses.

The new term in the solution for $\bar{p}_N$ can be understood in the light of the differing tax treatments of insurers and mutual funds. Unlike an insurer, a mutual fund is not taxed on any of its investment income. For the insurer, the larger the tax rate applied to its portfolio earnings, the larger the contribution that is required from the profit margin as an offset. The added term is not, however, quantitatively very important. For recent typical parameter values of t, s, and $\bar{r}_f$ given below, the new term adds only a little over one percentage point to the profit margin.[14]

If significant variations in the value of $\bar{p}_N$ did occur from firm to firm owing to dependence on parameters t and s, then firms' premiums would vary accordingly.[15] However, under perfect competition in the market for insurance, assuming in particular perfectly informed consumers, such differences, except as they related to product quality, would not survive. For the same reason, where rates are set by the state, regulators would probably not want to set different rates for different companies unless the differences related to quality.[16] Under competition, firms could only maintain equilibrium combinations of values of t and of s that yielded the same value for the added term and therefore for $\bar{p}_N$ and for premiums. Similar observations hold for possible interfirm differences in values of $\beta_{p,N}$. While industry averages of parameter values are used in the numerical profit solution shown below, it should be understood that the subject of insurance rate regulation, given substantial interfirm variations in all components of the rates, merits considerably more attention. This is true not only for purposes of asking how rates set by the state should be determined, but also in considering the case for open competition in pricing and in understanding how competition in the market would best work.

Effect of Regulation on Systematic Risk

Presumably regulation itself has some effect on the systematic risk of underwriting and therefore, through the estimated values of $\beta_{p,N}$, on required profit margins. These facts create a potential difficulty for regulatory use of these margins as profit factors if changes in the margins should lead to changes in the systematic risk in such a way that reestimation and resetting of margins produce sizeable and nonconverging values for the margins. However, in the light of the nonbinding nature of insurance margins, as is discussed below, it is questionable that the adoption of new margins would be likely to have much effect on systematic risks.

Numerical Profit Solutions

Required Profit Margins by Line

Numerical estimates of the required margins, given by equation (1.11a), depend upon the values of parameters expected to prevail in the policy year for which they are determined. For illustrative purposes the policy year has been chosen to be the calendar year 1977, and the estimation of all parameters is considered as of the end of 1976. Parameter estimates given here are believed to be reasonably illustrative values as of that time. Where better estimates for a policy year are available, they can, of course, be substituted for those chosen here.

Values of k_N are characteristic of the lines and will generally change little from year to year. They were determined from cash flows by line submitted to the Massachusetts Insurance Department. For $\bar{r}_f$ the one-year government-bond yield chosen is the 1976 year-end figure of 6 percent (rounded), which also happens to have been the average value for 1971–1975. For $\bar{r}_m - \bar{r}_f$, the average market risk premium, the Ibbotson and Sinquefield (1976) estimate of 8.8 percent is used. It is the average value for the period 1926–1974.

The average all-lines beta for liabilities, β_L, is estimated from samples of multiline insurers. Two methods of estimation have been used. Massachusetts Division of Insurance (1976a,b, 1977, and 1978) used the identity among the betas given by equation (1.6) to estimate β_L. The after-tax version of (1.6), after substituting $k\beta_L$ for β_p by virtue of (1.5), is

$$\beta_E = (1 - t)[\beta_A(ks + 1) - k\beta_L s] \tag{1.6a}$$

An estimate of β_L is obtained by solving equation (1.6a) for β_L and substituting estimates of parameters. Average industry values of t, s, β_A, and β_E in (1.6a) were estimated by using a sample consisting of the nine predominantly property-liability stock insurance companies in the *Value Line Investment Survey* (1976). *Value Line* is the only source of published data that provides periodic estimates of both betas and financial quantities for property-liability insurers. The parameter estimates are pooled average values for the nine companies over the period 1971–1975. They are: t equal to 0.2, s equal to 1.3, and β_E equal to 1.0, all rounded to one decimal place. The beta coefficient per dollar of assets, β_A, is a weighted average of betas for the different securities in company portfolios. Betas for the portfolios were estimated using a subsample of the *Value Line* companies for which portfolio composition was available. The estimated value for β_A is 0.5. Finally, an average value for the investable funds per dollar of premiums, k, was determined from the *Value Line* sample for 1971–1975 to be 0.8. Substituting all of the parameter estimates in (1.6a) yielded an estimate for β_L of −0.21.

Hill (1978) used a sample of six companies, substantially all of whose business was property-liability insurance, which reported the market value of bond holdings and were financed entirely by equity. Data on annual market-valued equity returns and annual market-valued investment returns were available for these firms for the period 1951 to 1965. Annual market-valued underwriting returns, r_L, were determined as the residual between return on equity and investment return. The beta for liabilities, β_L, was estimated by regressing the returns r_L on an overall market index r_m. The pooled-regression estimate for β_L for all companies for the period is −0.23 with a standard error of 0.24.[17] The simple average of six company betas estimated separately is −0.20.

It follows immediately from equation (1.1a) that both methods of estimating β_L would yield identical estimates if applied to a common sample of returns. Regression estimation has the advantages of supplying measures of precision of estimated parameters and avoiding possible selection biases in determining parameter values from separate data sources. The first method can be used when all the needed data series of annual returns are not available for a sample of companies, but estimates of parameter values can be determined separately.[18]

The closeness of the two estimates of β_L based on different samples is certainly supportive of the accuracy of each, but the sources of variability are clearly sufficiently large that the match must in part be coincidental. It is of some descriptive interest to note that "accounting betas" for liabilities or for underwriting determined by regressing annual-accounting underwriting returns against annual market-index returns are generally near zero in absolute value, although the possible downward bias in these estimates makes them suspect as estimates of true market betas.

The conclusion to be drawn from the available estimates of the systematic risks of underwriting profits for the major property-liability lines is that they are small in absolute value and are more likely to be positive than negative. Their absolute magnitudes, however, are subject to considerable uncertainty.

Estimates of $\beta_{p,N}$ by line are determined from equation (1.7) by substituting an industry all-lines estimate of β_L and the value of k_N by line. Using the estimate of $\beta_L = -0.21$ and values of k_N given in table 1-1 yields the following estimates of $\beta_{p,N}$ for five lines: for auto bodily injury, 0.34; for auto property damage, 0.07; for homeowners, 0.07; for workers' compensation, 0.34; and for medical malpractice, 0.79.

Required margins by line can now be determined by substituting estimated values of the parameters in equation (1.11), as modified slightly by a discounting factor that arises in the more detailed accounting given in an appendix available from the author. The margins so computed, $\bar{p}_{T,N}$, are close in value to and have essentially the same qualitative properties discussed for the $\bar{p}_N$. Table 1-2 gives the required margins for the major lines and medical malpractice, together with the traditional allowances. These new margins have a premium-weighted average level of −2.9 percent, which is 6.6 percentage points below the average level of 3.7 percent for the traditional margins.

The expected overall return on equity of insurers is near the average for U.S. industry, even with a negative average underwriting-profit level. Specifically, using the parameter values estimated above from *Value Line*, the industry beta on equity, β_E, is about 1, and if a company wrote just the four major lines represented in table 1-2 and had the 1975 national proportions of earned premiums, then, applying expression (1.1a) for $\bar{r}_E$, it would have had an estimated expected return of 15.4 percent as of the autumn of 1976.

Comparisons of CAPM Required and Traditional "Target" Margins with Historical Profit

The standard source of national insurance-industry statistics in the U.S. is *Best's Aggregates and Averages*. It reports underwriting profit and loss by line for stock insurers by calendar year of coverage. These profit and loss figures are based upon estimated claims and expenses as reported to state

Table 1-2. Profit Margins: CAPM Required; Traditional; and Historical (percent of premiums)

Line of Insurance	*(1) CAPM Required Margins (1977)*	*(2) Traditional "Target" Margins (Massachusetts)*	*(3) Historical Margins (1956–1975)*	*(4) Historical Margins (1971–1975)*
Auto bodily injury	−6.0%	1.0%[a]	−5.6%	−5.3%
Auto property damage	−0.1	5.0	−1.6	−1.2
Homeowners	−0.3	6.0	−9.7	−0.4
Workers' compensation[b]	−6.3	2.5	−2.3	−6.4
Weighted average	−2.9	3.7	−4.0	−3.2

[a] A 5 percent margin is customary in most states.

[b] Profit or loss as a percent of earned premiums is less estimated dividends of participating companies.

Sources: (3) and (4)—Best (1976) for years 1966–1975; auto lines' margins adjusted to Massachusetts categories and U.S. Department of Commerce, *Historical Statistics of the United States*, 1975, for years 1956–1965, adjusted.

insurance officials. Table 1-2 gives average historical margins for stock property-liability insurers in the United States as reported by Best (1976) for the recent five-year period 1971–1975 and the recent twenty-year period 1956–1975.[19]

The CAPM-required margins are close to historical average margins both in 1971–1975 and in 1956–1975. Their average is −2.9 percent, while the historical average margin for these four lines was −3.2 percent in 1971–1975 and −4.01 in 1956–1976. In contrast, the traditional "target" profit margins are uniformly higher than the same historical margins. The weighted average of the traditional target allowances is 3.7 percent, 6.9 percentage points higher than the corresponding 1971–1975 average realized margin, and 7.7 percentage points higher than the 1956–1975 average.

Implications for Rate Regulation

Bias in Traditional Profit Factors

It is widely acknowledged that the traditional target underwriting-profit margins are unsupported by any reasonable financial theory. The CAPM-required margins have an average level some 7 percentage points of premium below the traditional values. If the new margins are more nearly correct, then the traditional values are not only unsupported but are substantially biased upwards. Additional and independent support for the existence of an upward bias comes from other perspectives too.

First, historically, in the United States property-liability insurance business, average underwriting-profit margins have generally been negative and not far from the margins derived here on theoretical grounds. The traditional factors have evidently not been binding (see below for further discussion). The financial facts of life—not unrecognized in the industry—are that money is made on investments, not on underwriting.

Second, if the average traditional factor of 3.9 percent of premiums were actually earned, then using parameter values estimated above from *Value Line*, the estimated anticipated rate of return on equity for the industry as of the autumn of 1976 would have been 23.4 percent. The latter value is about 50 percent larger than the average for all U.S. industry, and some 7 or 8 percentage points above rates of return commonly granted to regulated public utilities like gas and electric services. The partially regulated property-liability industry is generally regarded as being of average riskiness, and a required return this high, while conceivable, would surprise most observers and require demonstration.[20]

Third, the traditional factors for underwriting profit are sometimes viewed as including a component to cover "contingencies" of rate inadequacies. If the expected value of this component is positive, it should be carried over into the accounting for the expected value of claims and expenses and not intermingled with a profit provision.

Nonbinding Official Factors

Historical underwriting margins have, as averages over time, failed to reach the levels contained in official rate filings before state commissioners. Evidently, the traditional target profit margins have not been binding. There are several possible explanations for this. For one, there is no established procedure for correcting the errors made in forecasts of profits. Insurance rate setting is generally prospective. It depends upon forecasts of future claims, expenses, and profits, and in most lines there is no customary provision for recoupment of losses nor, with few exceptions, for rebate of profits in excess of forecasted amounts.[21] Further, not only are there not mechanisms, typically, for actual financial reversal of errors, but after-the-fact analysis of forecasting errors is rare. Actuarial analysis as applied in actual rate filings has focused almost exclusively on the preparation of detailed accounting estimates in making forecasts of rate components. Such an analysis is in contradistinction to the fitting of specified statistical models in which parameter uncertainties and forecast errors are studied by using a sample of historical data.[22]

Another reason that a bias between forecasted and realized profit figures could persist uncorrected for a long time is that the realized underwriting-profit margin is highly variable. In the auto lines, for example, in periods of two to three years changes in the national margins have been as much as 10 to 15 percentage points and have gone from positive to negative and vice versa. Given the magnitudes of these fluctuations, it is less surprising than it might otherwise appear that a bias would be unremarked.

Explanations of the bias in the estimates that are founded upon possible strategic advantages in hearings or negotiations on rate filings can be put forward but are necessarily conjectural. One such explanation is that, when they can secure it, companies find it convenient to have one component in a rate filing with a generous upward margin as a buffer against low estimates of other components. Thus, when a strict review of rate filings brings estimates of claims or expenses below levels sought, the underwriting margin could make up for the difference. This explanation is consistent with the view of profit margins as part contingency loading.

An upward bias in official target profit margins provides an opportunity for the industry to earn profits—in excess of those needed (ex ante) to achieve the target rate of return. Whether, in fact, excessive profits are earned is, however, quite a different question, because rate competition, to the degree that it is effective, should force actual profits toward required levels. The historical record of margins some 7 or 8 points below traditional target margins on average must reflect such market pressures. The average level of the required margins derived here is close to the average level of historical margins. The prevalent view of independent observers is generally that the industry has probably not been earning large, excessive profits on average, though regulation may have kept profits somewhat above competitive levels. It appears that market forces have been a much more potent influence on profit outcomes than the numbers entered in official rate filings might lead one to expect.

Effect of Adopting New Required Margins

What would be the effect on actual profits of replacing the traditional target margins, which have averaged 3 to 4 percent in the major lines, with the new required margins proposed in this chapter, which have averaged around −3 percent?

It seems likely that in most states the effect would be only a paper change in rate filings and would have no net effect on actual profits. New official margins would replace the biased estimates with unbiased or less biased estimates. Other components of the rate filing would be reestimated in an upward direction to achieve the premium levels thought necessary. The reestimation would in most cases probably go unremarked because new rate filings submitted periodically contain numerous points at which subjective judgments are made about data sources, periods, methods of projection, etc. In fact, the available evidence indicates that such reestimation is required. If present rate levels are nearly correct, but profits are overestimated in the rates, then the other components of the rate level—claims and expenses—are underestimated. Such underestimation will not be present every year or necessarily in every state, but a persistent bias on the order of 6 or 7 percent—the mirror image of the profit overestimate—is suggested nationally.

Adoption of new profit margins would appear to have at most a transitory impact on the existing pattern by state and by line of net rate setting errors. That pattern, where rates are set or sanctioned by the state, is presumably the net result of contending adversarial forces. These errors, whether of underestimation (inadequacy) or overestimation (excessiveness), have generally undesired income-distributional and supply-side effects. Overestimates in the rates are burdensome to consumers. Underestimates hurt equity owners and affect the supply of capital. Market distortions resulting from these errors are certainly of concern. For example, if rates are not adequate, a variety of supply-side responses by companies that might well harm consumer welfare can be hypothesized—though the effects will depend on state laws. One response might be to set higher rates in other lines or in other states. Another would be to restrict books of business to the better risks and to discourage new applicants, or to place them into the assigned-risk or reinsurance pool. Important and unsettled questions of economic efficiency and welfare under uncertainty are raised in considering rate setting errors, whatever their direction, and they lead to larger questions of the scope of state or federal regulation and the role of competitive market alternatives.

Consideration of systematic risks, rates of return, and profit margins should be of interest whatever the form of market organization in a state. Rate filings before state commissioners of insurance too often fail to reflect either relevant economic and financial theory or empirical validation of methods and forecasts. The profit margins determined here are put forward as a step away from the routine use of unexamined figures and toward a deeper understanding of industry structure and of appropriate economic policy with regard to insurance pricing.

Notes

1. For decades the investment-income controversy has divided most of the property-liability insurance industry from those state regulators and consumer groups who would bring the investment returns of companies into the determination of appropriate price levels for insurance coverages. Insurers have argued, though perhaps with less unanimity in the last several years, that the sums earned from the investment of insureds' funds before their payout in claims and expenses are, in essence, part of another business and not the business of insurance per se. Opponents of the customary industry view have argued that this bifurcated view served only to conceal and protect lucrative investment earnings from public scrutiny and thereby to maintain insurance prices at higher levels than they would be if the investment side of the business were examined.

2. The National Association of Insurance Commissioners (1970) and Cooper (1974) give extensive historical background on the investment income controversy.

3. "[T]he return to the equity owner should be commensurate with returns on investments in other enterprises having corresponding risk." *Federal Power Commission v. Hope Natural Gas Co.*, 320 U.S. 591, 603 (1944). See also *Federal Power Commission v. Natural Gas*

Pipeline Co., 315 U.S. 575, 590, 596–8 (1942).

4. In the late 1960s the insurance industry commissioned studies on profitability by Arthur D. Little (ADL). See Arthur D. Little (1970) and Plotkin (1969). The ADL studies examined rates of return to book equity. Their choice of book equity created serious measurement issues, but their principal problem was reliance on an unestablished risk-return theory. See Joskow 1973, pp. 417–420 and Hill 1978, pp. 30–32.

5. At the December 1975 hearings on auto insurance rates in Massachusetts, three academic experts in finance testified: Professors Fisher Black and Eli Shapiro of the Sloan School of Business of the Massachusetts Institute of Technology and Professor Peter Jones of the Harvard Business School. All three agreed that a rate-of-return standard was appropriate for determining underwriting margins for use in rate setting and that the target rate of return should be determined by applying the CAPM.

6. *Attorney General v. Commissioner of Insurance*, 353 N.E. 2d 745 (1976).

7. In many states, for example, a consumer who fails to find auto insurance in the voluntary market can only purchase coverage at much higher prices and with limited options in an assigned-risk pool or reinsurance facility. By contrast, in Massachusetts customers whom private carriers choose to reinsure through the reinsurance facility must by law, and with minor exceptions, be treated exactly like others as to price and service. Like others, too, they pay premium surcharges as they incur at-fault claims or moving violations. The point here is not whether Massachusetts' laws in this area are wise but that the actual effects of changing books of business depend on the entire statutory framework in a state.

8. In the simplest capital-market equilibrium framework, a theorem is that all investors invest in the market portfolio. An insurer, however, as a financial intermediary, need not select the market portfolio even within the simple framework. Hence, $\bar{r}_A$ can differ between insurers, and in practice it does. I am indebted to Raymond D. Hill for this observation.

9. Myers (1972) discusses the *Hope* decision and its capital-attraction standard.

10. Auto insurance coverages are usually classified as "liability" or "physical damage." Massachusetts' "bodily injury" coverages are all "liability." Massachusetts' property-damage coverages, with the exception of property-damage liability, are "physical damage."

11. By the definition of a beta coefficient, the value of β_p measures the change in underwriting profits associated with a change in the overall market index. Similarly, β_L measures the change in the value of liabilities associated with a change in the index.

12. Biger and Kahane (1978) make a specific suggestion.

13. Commissioner Robert L. Clifford's decision on auto rates (1972) is the basis for the New Jersey method.

14. The premium-to-capital ratio, s, is treated as exogenous in the present analysis. Further work on the role of s is called for, notably in relation to possible anticipatory behavior by firms and the effect on insolvency probability.

15. Varying t and s between ranges of observed values for a sample of nine insurers discussed below produces variations in the added term of about a percentage point. These interfirm variations are in contrast to larger ones present in expenses and claims. For example, the twenty largest writers of auto insurance in Massachusetts filed rate filings with the Insurance Department for the year 1977 listing expense ratios for auto liability coverages which varied between 25.6 percent and 42.3 percent and for physical damage coverages between 22.4 percent and 35.7 percent. While some part of these ranges might be explained by differences in accounting conventions, in particular interstate cost allocations, they are still likely to be indicative of substantial variation from other sources.

16. In Massachusetts, Commissioner James M. Stone (1975) proposed the use of a hypothetical insurance company that invested only in U.S. government bonds to determine a

maximum profit factor for all companies. Cooper (1974) had made a similar proposal independently. The idea is that any real company can do at least as well in anticipated investment returns as the hypothetical company, but that the profit factor of a real company—and therefore the consumer's premium—should be no greater on account of the investment risks it voluntarily undertakes. The hypothetical company can be called the "regulatory standard company" (Massachusetts Division of Insurance 1976a, b, 1977). The form of the profit-margin solution given by expression (1.11) in the text is the same for the regulatory standard company as for any other. However, a difference in numerical results does emerge when corporate taxes on earnings of around 20 percent are taken into account. Regulatory standard companies investing in U.S. government bonds would be taxed at the full corporate rate of 46 percent. The use of the higher rate raises required profits by about 3 percent. Tax incentives therefore favor a diversified portfolio and not that of the regulatory standard company. This observation probably explains why such companies are rare in the real world.

17. That the estimated coefficient is not statistically significant at the usual levels of a *t*-test is not critical here. In the decision-making context of rate determination or rate review, only if there were strong prior probability attached to a null value (like zero), or if the loss function on the errors of estimation favored avoidance of error at a null value, might that value be chosen over the observed value. In the present instance there is some prior-probability weight attached to values of B_L near zero, and a Bayesian estimate that took this into account would be somewhat closer to zero. Study of the error structure would be of interest, but for the present it is assumed to be symmetrical.

18. In principle, the use of an identity can give a smaller standard error of the estimate than regression, if the parameter estimates substituted in it are more precise than the corresponding regression estimates of these parameters. Also, data-based measures of precision could be developed. Mosteller and Tukey (1977) give examples of these for situations where model-based estimates are not credible.

19. The underwriting profit margin as reported by Best (1976) is the statutory underwriting gain or loss (premiums earned less losses and expenses incurred) as a ratio to premiums earned. The low value for homeowners insurance in 1956–1975 reflects extremely large losses in the first years. The line is new and Best's reports profit margins for it only since 1955. Apparently the initial pricing of the line for a select low-risk group was far below claims costs that appeared when demand for the line increased.

20. In a monograph on the role of investment income in property-liability rates, Cooper (1974) studied risk-return relationships in the industry. His use of total variability of returns as the measure of risk is not consistent with the CAPM and leads to different analytical solutions for profit margins, but his numerical solutions are negative and closer to those derived here than to the traditional factors.

21. Williams (1978) reviews state "excess profits" statutes.

22. Chang and Fairley (1979) give an extended illustration and discussion of a traditional rate-setting method as contrasted with an approach drawing on statistical models and estimation theory.

References

Arthur D. Little Co. 1970. *Studies in the Profitability, Industrial Structure, Finance, and Solvency of the Property and Liability Insurance Industry*. Report to the

Insurance Rating Board. June 15.

Best, Company, A.M. 1976. *Best's Aggregates and Averages*. Property-Casualty.

Bicksler, J.L. 1976. South Carolina Public Service Commission, Docket No. 76-352-C, Southern Bell.

Biger, N., and Y. Kahane. 1978. Risk considerations in insurance ratemaking. *Journal of Risk and Insurance* 45(March):121–132.

Black, E. 1975. Testimony at hearings on 1976 automobile insurance rates. Massachusetts Division of Insurance. (December): Transcript pp. 16-135–16-161.

Brigham, E.F. 1977. Testimony, Public Utility Commission of Oregon.

Chang, L., and W.B. Fairley. 1979. Pricing automobile insurance under multivariate classification of risks: Additive versus multiplicative. *Journal of Risk and Insurance* 46(March):75–93.

Clifford, R.L. (Commissioner of Insurance, New Jersey). 1972. Determination on Automobile Rates. February 3.

Cooper, R.W. 1974. *Investment Return and Property-Liability Insurance Ratemaking*. Homewood, Ill.: Richard D. Irwin.

Fama, E.F. 1977. Risk-adjusted discount rates and capital budgeting under uncertainty. *Journal of Financial Economics* (5)August:3–24.

Finkelstein, M.O. 1973. Regression models in administrative proceedings. *Harvard Law Review* 86(June):1442–1475.

Forbes. 1975. 27th Annual Report on American Industry. 115(January 1):119–229.

Hill, R.D. 1978. Capital market equilibrium and the regulation of property-liability insurance. Unpublished Ph.D. dissertation, Department of Economics, Massachusetts Institute of Technology. April.

Ibbotson, R.G., and R.A. Sinquefield. 1976. Stocks, bonds, bills, and inflation: Year-by-year historical returns (1926–1974). *Journal of Business* 49(January): 11–47.

Jensen, M.C. (Ed.) 1972. *Studies in the Theory of Capital Markets*. New York: Praeger.

Joskow, P.L. 1973. Cartels, competition, and regulation in the property-liability insurance industry. *Bell Journal of Economics* 4(Autumn):375–427.

Macauley, F.R. 1938. *Some Theoretical Problems Suggested by the Movements of Interest Rates, Bond Yields, and Stock Prices in the United States Since 1856*. New York: National Bureau of Economic Research.

Massachusetts Division of Insurance, State Rating Bureau. 1976a. Rate of return and profit provision in medical malpractice insurance. December 1.

Massachusetts Division of Insurance, State Rating Bureau. 1976b. Rate of return and profit provision in automobile insurance. December 20.

Massachusetts Division of Insurance, State Rating Bureau. 1977. Rate of return and profit provision in workers' compensation. November 4.

Massachusetts Division of Insurance, State Rating Bureau. 1978. The investment income controversy and the regulation of profit in property-liability insurance. April 18.

Mosteller, F., and J.W. Tukey. 1977. *Data Analysis and Regression*. New York: Addison-Wesley.

Munch, P., and D. Smallwood. 1978. Solvency regulation in the property-casualty insurance industry. Santa Monica: Rand Corporation.

Myers, S.C. 1972a. The application of finance theory in public utility rate cases. *Bell Journal of Economics* 3(Spring):58–97.

Myers, S.C. 1972b. On the use of beta in regulatory proceedings: A comment. *Bell Journal of Economics* 3(Autumn):622–627.

Myers, S.C., and S.M. Turnbull. Capital budgeting and the capital asset pricing model: Good news and bad news. *Journal of Finance* 32(May):321–333.

National Association of Insurance Commissioners. 1970. Measurement of profitability and treatment of investment income in property and liability insurance. *Proceedings of the NAIC.*

Peseau, D.E., and T.M. Zepp. 1978. On the use of the CAPM in public utility rate cases: Comment. *Financial Management* 7(Autumn):52–56.

Pettway, R.H. 1978. On the use of beta in regulatory proceedings: An empirical examination. *Bell Journal of Economics* 9(Spring):239–248.

Plotkin, I.H. 1969. Rates of return in the property and liability insurance industry: A comparative analysis. *Journal of Risk and Insurance* 36(June):173–200.

Quirin, G.D., and W.R. Waters. 1975. "Market efficiency and the cost of capital: The strange case of fire and casualty insurance companies." *Journal of Finance* 30(May):427–450.

Robichek, A.A. 1978. Regulation and modern finance theory. *Journal of Finance* 33(June):693–705.

Ross, S.A. 1978. The current status of the capital asset pricing model (CAPM). *Journal of Finance* 33(June):885–901.

Stone, J.M. (Commissioner of Insurance, Massachusetts). 1975a. Opinions, findings, and decision on workmen's compensation rates. May.

Stone, J.M. (Commissioner of Insurance, Massachusetts). 1975b. Opinions, findings, and decision on 1976 automobile bodily injury coverage rates. November.

Stone, J.M. (Commissioner of Insurance, Massachusetts). 1975c. Opinions, findings, and decision on 1976 automobile property damage coverage rates. December.

Value Line Investment Survey. 1976. New York: Value Line, Inc. June 25.

2 THE MASSACHUSETTS MODEL OF PROFIT REGULATION IN NONLIFE INSURANCE: AN APPRAISAL AND EXTENSIONS

Raymond D. Hill and Franco Modigliani

In the late 1970s, a number of economists applied the Capital Asset Pricing Model (CAPM) to the problem of pricing insurance contracts (e.g., Munch and Smallwood 1978, Fairley, 1979, and Hill 1979). The CAPM offered a means of systematically accounting for the investment income of insurance companies and an operational definition of the risk of underwriting. In 1977, William Fairley used the CAPM to build a model for the regulatory determination of profit margins in Massachusetts. The Fairley model has played a major role in rate hearings in Massachusetts since its introduction. It has become generally known as the "Massachusetts" model of profit regulation. The purpose of this chapter is to provide a critical appraisal of the use of the Fairley model as a regulatory tool. The theoretical foundations of the model are reviewed, several extensions of its basic specification are suggested, and additional empirical evidence on its reliability and stability is provided.

The appraisal begins with a review of what the Fairley model attempts to do and the logic behind its approach. Specifically, the steps that lead to estimation of the risk of underwriting are outlined, and the use of current Treasury bill rates to measure investment income is discussed. Two simplifying assumptions made by Fairley that have potentially significant

---

Editor's Note: This chapter is an edited version of a paper dated August 1981 that was prepared for the 1982 Massachusetts automobile rate hearings.

consequences are then considered in detail: the taxation of insurance company income and the treatment of insurance company investments in assets which are not actively traded on securities markets. In both cases, new results are derived and new empirical evidence is provided. The taxation results have implications for virtually any rate of return model for insurance.

The analysis next considers the empirical application of the Fairley model. The amount of data available for estimation of the systematic risk of insurance is expanded relative to previous work. The stability of the model's estimates over time and the sensitivity of the estimates to assumptions about the values of certain parameters are examined.

The final issue examined is the sensitivity of the model to inflation. The specification is extended to examine the question of whether the risk of a particular line of insurance is proportional to the period over which claims are paid. The chapter concludes with a few observations about the advantages of using the Fairley model to regulate rates.

An Overview of the Fairley Model

This section provides a general description of the Fairley model and briefly discusses the sources of the key parameters. The precise algebraic formulation of the model appears in subsequent sections along with the modification proposed in this study.

The regulation of profitability in the nonlife insurance industry has traditionally focused on the profit margin per dollar of sales. If the timing of receipts and expenditures is ignored, the profit margin has the convenient economic interpretation of being a risk premium per dollar of expected loss (since premiums are roughly proportional to expected losses). However, ignoring the timing of receipts and expenditures is a significant omission, since the ability to earn investment income on the delay between premium receipts and loss payments is an important source of revenue in the insurance business.

The aim of the Fairley model was to solve for a profit rate which reflected the potential investment income available from the cash flow generated by the insurance. Such a profit margin could replace the traditional and arbitrary fixed profit margin per dollar of sales, p, which is defined without any reference to the timing of flows:

$$p = (\mathrm{P} - \bar{L})/P \tag{2.1}$$

where P is the premium and L the expected loss per policy. (For simplicity, expense loadings are not considered in this discussion.) The problem, once the timing of the cash flow is recognized, is to find the value of p which, when combined with investment income, insures a return on equity that includes a risk premium that fairly compensates insurance company owners.

Fairley calculates the fair risk premium by using the Sharpe-Lintner Capital Asset Pricing Model (CAPM) to provide a definition of risk and an empirically computable relationship between risk and return.[1] Fairley decomposed the overall risk of the firm into two parts:

risk of the firm = risk of the investment portfolio + risk of underwriting

The overall risk of the firm can be measured from the variability of its stock return. Since the investment portfolio consists largely of actively traded assets, its risk also can be measured, at least approximately. Thus, although the risk of underwriting cannot be observed, it can be calculated from the above relationship and used to calculate the fair risk premium per dollar of insurance.

In practice, the risk of underwriting must be inferred from a limited sample of companies: those whose business is only (or predominantly) nonlife insurance and who have shares actively traded on the stock exchanges. For this study, these constraints produced a sample of 10 firms categorized as nonlife companies by *Value Line*.

Two additional assumptions underlie Fairley's derivation. The first is that the risk of underwriting varies among lines of insurance only in proportion to the length of the period over which claims are paid. For example, if workers' compensation claims take twice as long to settle on average as automobile liability claims, the risk of the former is assumed to be twice as high as the risk of the latter.

The second assumption is that the risk of underwriting does not vary significantly across firms—or, at a minimum, that the average risk of the *Value Line* sample is close to the average for all firms under regulation. Note that the overall risk of the firm varies considerably across firms since it depends on the firm's leverage (i.e., the ratio of invested assets to equity), the composition of the investment portfolio (proportion of "safe" bonds vs. "risky" stocks), and the rate at which the firm pays taxes (the higher the tax rate the more the U.S. Treasury shares in the firm's risk).[2] Each of these sources of variation in firm risk can be controlled for, however, so that they do not affect the measurement of underwriting risk.

An example may help to illustrate this point. In general, it is well known (e.g., Hamada 1972) that a firm's risk depends on its financial structure. Thus, while the manufacture of steel may be assumed to have approximately the same risk whether carried out by the Bethlehem Steel Company or by Republic Steel, if Bethlehem operates at a higher level of financial leverage (a higher debt/equity ratio) than Republic, the risk of Bethlehem's stock also will be higher. Rosenberg and Guy (1976a, b) have used this property to predict changes in the risk of firms. By controlling for changes in such variables as leverage, they are better able to measure the constant part of a firm's risk, which presumably reflects its underlying business risk. Their procedure is very close to that followed in the Fairley model. By accounting for changes in the ratio of assets to equity, in the composition of the investment portfolio, and in taxation, the model isolates the risk of underwriting that may be relatively stable across firms and over time.

Once the risk of underwriting is measured, the fair risk premium can be computed. An allowance for investment income is then deducted from this risk premium. The Fairley model uses Treasury bill rates to impute investment income to the firm. Normally, Treasury bills represent bonds with the lowest yields, because of their low risk.[3] When this study was conducted, however, there was an "inverted" yield curve; that is, bonds with very short maturities had higher yields than did long-term bonds.

An inverted yield curve generally reflects abnormally high short-term rates and expectations that interest rates will fall in the future. When the yield curve is inverted, the use of Treasury bill rates to impute investment income may appear to overstate the investment income available to insurance firms. This appearance is compounded by the fact that companies report income based on "embedded" bond yields; that is, the actual coupon rates available when the bonds were purchased rather than current market yields. Since yields have risen over the last decade, current Treasury bill rates are higher than the yields insurance companies report in their financial statements.

The Fairley model's use of Treasury bill rates to impute investment income can be defended on a number of grounds. First, current market yields should always be used in preference to embedded or trended (a common actuarial practice) yields. Investors are interested in what they will earn on currently invested assets, not in past history. The practical effect of using embedded yields is to understate the profitability of insurance when yields are rising and to overstate it when yields are falling. Only current yields will insure that regulation meets a "capital attraction" standard at all times.

Second, the use of Treasury bill rates insulates policyholders from the risk of insurance company investments. In a competitive market, an insurance company that tried to recoup past investment losses by charging current policyholders higher premiums would rapidly lose business. New entrants, not burdened with those losses, would be able to charge lower prices and still provide an attractive return to their invested capital. Insurance companies may purchase long-term bonds or stocks if they believe their returns will be higher than those on Treasury bills. Under the Fairley model, if such expectations are realized, the stockholders will enjoy higher returns as a reward for investing in riskier, long-term assets. However, if the expectations are not realized, it also is the stockholders who will suffer the loss—not the policyholders through higher premiums.

A third advantage of using Treasury bill yields is that they are closely tied to expectations about short-term inflation. The profit rate essentially is calculated as a percentage of expected losses and expenses that is implicitly adjusted for future inflation. Thus, the use of Treasury bills may help to insure that the real value of the risk premium is maintained.[4]

This broad overview of the Fairley model indicates that the general approach is relatively straightforward and uncomplicated. When applying the model in practice, however, a number of complicating issues arise. The remainder of this chapter focuses on several of these issues.

The Treatment of Taxes

The profit margin set by the commissioner must include an allowance for federal income taxes paid by insurance firms. The appropriate allowance for taxes has been subject to considerable dispute in past hearings in Massachusetts. Three principal questions have been raised in this debate.

First, Fairley's model assumed that a single average tax rate was applied to the firm's income. In fact, underwriting income and various classes of investment income are taxed at different rates. The question arises as to whether the model should be amended to reflect the more complicated nature of reality, and, if so, the form that the modifications should take.

Second, when the profit margin is negative, the higher the tax rate that is assumed on underwriting, the lower is the required profit margin calculated by the Fairley model. This occurs because negative underwriting results can shield positive income from other sources. The higher the tax rate used, the more one assumes underwriting losses are offset by tax savings. A single tax rate implies that the tax burden on positive income is at the same rate as the tax shield associated with losses. In his 1981 rate decision, the Commissioner assumed that negative underwriting income was taxed at a zero rate—i.e., no positive income was shielded. The rationale for this decision was that a firm writing only in Massachusetts and making negative underwriting income would have no positive profits to shield. The question arises as to whether this assumption is appropriate.

The argument also has been made that the use of any tax rate relying on the average experience of real firms is inconsistent with the Fairley model's use of the Treasury bill rate to impute investment income. Since interest on Treasury bills is taxed at the corporate tax rate, the argument goes, it is illogical to use anything but the 46 percent tax rate in the profit formula. The third question concerns the validity of this argument. In order to help answer these questions, an explicit formula for the taxes paid by an insurance firm is needed.

The Taxation of Insurance Company Income

The total reported income of the firm is taxed at the corporate income tax rate (currently 46 percent). However, investment income is effectively taxed at different rates because different proportions of different types of investment income are taxable. Let v_j represent the proportion of income of type j on which tax is paid. There are typically four types of income:

1. Taxable interest: $v_1 = 1.0$ (i.e., 100 percent taxable)
2. Capital gains:[5] $v_2 = 0.61$
3. Dividends: $v_3 = 0.15$
4. Tax-exempt interest: $v_4 = 0.0$

Henceforth, we will refer to taxable investment income as that portion actually subject to tax, given the weights above.

Let T equal total taxes paid by the firm; w_j equal the weight of the asset producing income of type j in the total portfolio; r_j equal the yield on income of type j; and t equal the corporate income tax rate (0.46).[6] In addition, let s be the ratio of (annual) premiums to surplus (where surplus is equivalent to equity or net worth) and k be the ratio of reserves to premiums (which will also measure the average delay in claim payments). Thus, $ks + 1$ represents assets per dollar of surplus (or equity).

The tax paid by the firm per dollar of equity will be

$$T = t\left[\sum_{j=1}^{4} w_j v_j r_j (ks + 1) + ps\right] \tag{2.2}$$

and the return to equity will be

$$r_E = (ks + 1)\left(\sum_j w_j r_j - t\sum_j w_j v_j r_j\right) + ps(1 - t) \tag{2.3}$$

as long as either the underwriting profit margin, p, is positive or total taxable investment income exceeds the underwriting loss. In the latter case, the absolute tax rate for underwriting income is 0.46 regardless of whether p is positive or negative. For example, positive underwriting profits of $100 would provide net income of $54; an underwriting loss of $100 would reduce taxes paid on investment income by $46 so the net loss would be $54.[7] Taxes on investment income per dollar of equity are given by $t(ks + 1)\Sigma_j w_j v_j r_j$. The term

$$t_a = \frac{t\sum_j w_j v_j r_j}{\sum_j w_j r_j} \tag{2.4}$$

represents the overall tax rate on investment income, that is, taxes paid per dollar of investment income for a given set of portfolio weights, w_j.

When the underwriting loss exceeds taxable investment income, then no taxes are paid. In the absence of loss carryovers, the value of the tax shield is

$$t\sum_j w_j v_j r_j (ks + 1)$$

regardless of the size of the underwriting loss. The return to equity is

$$r_E = (ks + 1)\sum_j w_j r_j + ps \tag{2.5}$$

Whether equation (2.3) or (2.5) is appropriate is an empirical question. The answer depends on the relative size of underwriting and investment income which, in turn, depends on the composition of the investment portfolio.

Analysis shown in Appendix 2A suggests that taxable investment income per dollar of assets for the typical Massachusetts firm in 1980 was no greater than 5.6 percent.[8] Combining this figure with the ratio of assets to premiums, a typical Massachusetts firm would pay some taxes at any underwriting margin higher than −8.43 percent. In other words, when the profit rate falls below −8.43 percent, underwriting losses exceed taxable investment income. For values of p greater than this figure, the effective tax rate (or value of the tax shield) for underwriting income remains the corporate tax rate.

The above analysis provides answers to the first two questions raised concerning tax rates. The Fairley model can be easily amended to account for different tax rates on investment and underwriting income. It also is clear that there is value to the tax shield of underwriting losses even if the firm never has positive underwriting income.

The Use of Treasury Bill Yields and Actual Taxes on Investment Income

The third question raised above, whether it is illogical to impute investment income at the yield on Treasury bills (which would be taxed at the 46 percent rate) but use tax rates based on the actual investment portfolio to calculate the allowed underwriting profit margin, can be answered by reviewing the derivation of the underwriting profit margin in the Fairley model. The model defines two rates of return to equity. One is the target rate, r_E^g, which is the "fair" return as defined by the CAPM. The second is the actual expected return to equity for the firm, $\bar{r}_E$. The actual return depends on the values of s, k, r_j, and the effective tax rates (i.e., on t, v_j, and w_j). The values used for these variables are average values for the set of firms being regulated. The Fairley model then solves for the underwriting profit margin which equates r_E^g and $\bar{r}_E$. The resulting profit margin produces a fair return, given the investment policy and tax rates of the average firm.

It can easily be shown that the use of actual tax rates on investment income in the Fairley model will produce expected returns to equity which are consistent with the equilibrium expected returns of the CAPM. If, instead, underwriting profit rates are derived under the assumption that firms are taxed at a 46 percent rate on investment income, expected returns to equity based on parameters specific to Massachusetts firms appear to exceed significantly reasonable target returns. Details are provided in Appendix 2B.

Taxes and the Beta of Underwriting

The revised treatment of taxes also needs to be incorporated into the calculation of the beta for the firm's liabilities. The tax rates used must be specific to the *Value Line* sample in order to distinguish clearly the risk of underwriting from the effects of taxes and leverage. The firms in the *Value Line* sample are sometimes in the situation described by equation (2.3) where taxable income is positive and sometimes in a situation described by equation (2.5) where no taxes are paid. Moreover, the underwriting income measure used for tax purposes that is based on statutory accounting rules tends to be systematically lower than the GAAP underwriting income measure that is used in regulatory proceedings.[9]

To calculate the beta of liabilities, a measure of the average relationship between taxes and the two income sources is needed. Such a relationship was estimated from the following regression:

$$T_{i,t} = \alpha_1 II_{i,t} + \alpha_2 UI_{i,t} + \varepsilon_{i,t}$$

where for the ith firm in year t, T is total taxes paid, II is before-tax investment income, and UI is before-tax (GAAP) underwriting income. From equations (2.2) and (2.4), it can be seen that α_1 is a measure of the average value of t_a and α_2 is the average tax on underwriting.

From ten years of data for the seven-firm sample described later in the chapter, the following results were obtained: $\hat{\alpha}_1 = 0.21$ and $\hat{\alpha}_2 = 0.24$.[10] These estimates are used in the derivation of the beta of liabilities shown below. A notable result is that the estimated average tax rate for underwriting income is significantly less than 0.46, even though the sample firms on average had positive underwriting income.

The Treatment of Nontraded Assets

One of the key steps in applying the Fairley model is the decomposition of the risk of the firm into the risk of its investments and the risk of its underwriting. Using the Sharpe-Lintner CAPM definition of risk, the beta of a firm's equity (β_E) must be a weighted average of the betas of its investment and underwriting activities. At any point in time, the value of its underwriting activities equals the expected value of claims to be paid in the future, or the expected value of liabilities. Hence,

$$\beta_E = \frac{V_A}{V_E}\beta_A - \frac{V_L}{V_E}\beta_L \tag{2.6}$$

where V_E, V_A, and V_L are the values of equity, assets, and liabilities, respectively; β_A is the beta of assets; and β_L is the beta of liabilities.

In order to calculate β_E, a more detailed specification of the return to equity (r_E) is needed. In Fairley's original one-tax rate formulation, r_E is given by

$$r_E = (1 - t)[(ks + 1)r_a + ps] \tag{2.7}$$

where r_a is the overall investment return on assets. The beta of liabilities, β_L, reflects the systematic risk of the underwriting profit rate, β_p. Assuming that the relationship between β_p and β_L is proportional to the average delay in claim payment so that $\beta_p = -k\beta_L$ implies that

$$\beta_E = (1 - t)[(ks + 1)\beta_A - ks\beta_L] \tag{2.8}$$

where k is the ratio of reserves to premiums. Solving equation (2.8) gives

$$\beta_L = \frac{ks + 1}{ks}\beta_A - \frac{1}{(1 - t)ks}\beta_E \tag{2.9}$$

In computing k, Fairley used the formula

$$k = \frac{\text{reserves}}{\text{premiums}} = \frac{\text{stocks} + \text{bonds} - V_E}{\text{premiums}} \tag{2.10}$$

This procedure assumes that all assets are either stocks or bonds. This is a convenient assumption, since the betas of actively traded stocks and bonds can be readily estimated. However, as table 2-1 illustrates, a nontrivial proportion of insurance company assets are "nontraded," that is, they are neither stocks nor bonds and are not actively traded on securities markets. This is true both for the *Value Line* sample and for the major insurance writers in Massachusetts. The question arises as to what effect incorrectly ignoring these assets has on the Fairley estimate of β_L.

To answer this question, retain Fairley's definition of k as given in equation (2.10), and let k_N be the ratio of nontraded assets to premiums. The beta of equity is now

$$\beta_E = \frac{V_A}{V_E}\beta_A + \frac{V_N}{V_E}\beta_N - \frac{V_L}{V_E}\beta_L$$

or, using the analogue to equation (2.7),

$$\beta_E = (1 - t)[(ks + 1)\beta_A + k_N s\beta_N - (k + k_N)s\beta_L] \tag{2.11}$$

Solving equation (2.11) for β_L gives

$$\beta_L = \frac{ks + 1}{(k + k_N)s}\beta_A + \frac{k_N}{(k + k_N)}\beta_N - \frac{1}{(1 - t)(k + k_N)s}\beta_E \tag{2.12}$$

Defining $\lambda = k/(k + k_N)$ gives

$$\beta_L = \lambda\left[\frac{ks + 1}{ks}\beta_A - \frac{1}{(1 - t)ks}\beta_E\right] + \lambda\beta_N\frac{k_N}{k} \tag{2.13}$$

Comparing equation (2.13) with equation (2.9), it can be seen that the effect of ignoring nontraded assets was to overstate the systematic risk of the underwriting profit rate. Fairley's estimate of β_L was negative. The correct estimate is some fraction ($\lambda < 1$) of that negative number plus a

Table 2-1. Size and Composition of Nontraded Asset Portfolios for *Value Line* Companies: 1980

Company	*Book Value of Nontraded Assets ($ million)*	*Nontraded Assets ÷ Total Assets*	*Receivables and Cash ÷ Nontraded Assets*	*Real Estate ÷ Nontraded Assets*	*Loans ÷ Nontraded Assets*
Crum and Forster	2723.1	.30	.15	.01	n.a.
GEICO Corp.	499.1	.34	.45	.10	.05
INA Corp.	4389.2	.41	.32	n.a.	.05
Ohio Casualty Corp.	73.8	.20	.65	.11	n.a.
Safeco Corp.	348.8	.44	.31	n.a.	.02
St. Paul Companies	1179.3	.28	.25	.01	n.a.
U.S. Fid. & Guar. Co.	547.7	.22	.60	.11	.01

Source: Moody's Bank and Finance Manual (1981). (No 1980 data in *Moody's* for Chubb, Continental, and Mission.)

term, $\lambda\beta_N k_N/k$, which will be positive as long as β_N is positive. Thus, β_L rises with the addition of nontraded assets. Since the systematic risk of the profit rate, β_p, is negatively related to β_L, it falls.

Data concerning the nature of nontraded assets are limited. Table 2-1 illustrates the composition of nontraded assets for the *Value Line* companies with information available in *Moody's Bank and Finance Manual*. The proportion of nontraded assets composed of cash and receivables should have virtually no systematic risk. The authors guess that loans and real estate each have a beta no greater than the 0.125 that is used as an estimate of the systematic risk of bonds in the work described in the next section. This suggests that a reasonable range for β_N is between zero and 0.125. In the next section, the sensitivity of β_L to different values of β_N is examined using the *Value Line* sample.

The preceding analysis has considered the addition of nontraded assets to Fairley's original one-tax model. For empirical estimation, a two-tax version is needed that combines these results with the earlier derivation of the two-tax model. With two tax rates and nontraded assets, an empirically tractable measure of β_E is given by

$$\beta_E = (1 - t_a)(ks + 1)\beta_A + (1 - t_a)k_N s\beta_N - (1 - t)(k + k_N)s\beta_L$$

Solving for β_L gives

$$\beta_L = \frac{(1 - t_a)(ks + 1)}{(1 - t)(k + k_N)s}\beta_A + \frac{(1 - t_a)k_N}{(1 - t)(k + k_N)}\beta_N - \frac{1}{(1 - t)(k + k_N)s}\beta_E \qquad (2.14)$$

This formula for β_L is used to obtain the results presented in the next section.

Empirical Estimates

New estimates of the systematic risk of underwriting based on a larger set of data than was used by Fairley and on the previously described extensions of the model are reported in this section. Illustrative profit rates reflecting these changes also are calculated.

The Risk of Underwriting

The systematic risk of underwriting profit rates is obtained from estimates of the beta of an insurance firm's liabilities (β_L). For his original estimates, Fairley used five years of data on nine firms. In this study, one firm was added to the Fairley sample and the fourteen-year time period from 1967 through 1980 was used. In doing so, the authors believe that they have exhausted the possibilities of using data from financial markets to infer the risk of underwriting. The new estimates of the systematic risk of underwriting obtained with these data are insensitive to the firms included in the sample and are relatively stable over time. By "relatively," the authors mean that the profit rates implied by various estimates of the risk of underwriting do not differ much in comparison, say, with changes induced by varying yields on investment income or with the observed variance in profit rates.

The data needed to estimate the beta of liabilities were taken for each firm from the *Value Line Investment Survey*. Any gaps or omissions were filled from the financial statements published in *Moody's Bank and Finance Manual*. The beta of equity (β_E) is the limiting factor in determining the size of the sample. *Value Line* did not begin publishing β_E until 1971. Moreover, β_E can only be estimated for firms whose stock is actively traded on the exchanges.

Value Line and Massachusetts Firms. Before presenting the systematic risk estimates, a few observations on the appropriateness of using figures from the *Value Line* sample to provide a measure of underwriting risk for Massachusetts firms are needed. Table 2-2 summarizes selected financial data for the *Value Line* sample and for seven of the ten largest writers in Massachusetts for which the relevant data were available in *Moody's Bank and Finance Manual.*[11] These seven firms represent about 40 percent of the Massachusetts auto market in terms of premiums written.

The firms in both samples are of roughly comparable size, and both sets of firms tend to write automobile insurance as only a moderate part of a diversified underwriting portfolio. In fact, the size of the firms in the Massachusetts sample is understated since a number of these companies are part of larger groups. Also, the fraction of the nonauto business for these larger groups would be larger.

As mentioned, the method of estimating β_L controls for differences in leverage and asset composition. Nevertheless, it is worth noting that the leverage for the *Value Line* firms is somewhat higher than for the Massachusetts firms. Also, while the composition of assets is broadly similar, the average proportion of nontraded assets is considerably higher for the *Value Line* sample. Additional comparisons by the authors indicated no clear pattern within the *Value Line* sample between size or the

Table 2-2. Selected Financial Data for the Major Insurance Writers in Massachusetts and the *Value Line* Companies: 1980

Company	*Net Premiums Written ($ million)*	*Auto Premiums ÷ Total Premiums*	*Assets ($ million)*	*Bonds ÷ Assets*	*Stocks ÷ Assets*	*Nontraded Assets ÷ Assets*	*Reserves ÷ Premiums*	*Premiums ÷ Surplus*
The Major Insurance Writers in Massachusetts:								
Aetna Cas. & Sur. Co.	3040.5	34%	6519.6	56%	19%	25%	1.6	2.5
Comm. Union Ins. Co.	725.8	n.a.	1348.0	55	22	23	1.2	2.5
Travelers Indemnity Co.	1844.8	35	4751.9	53	17	30	1.6	1.6
Liberty Mutual Ins. Co.	2580.7	33	5605.7	77	7	16	1.7	2.6
Sentry Ins.-A Mut. Co.	283.8	33	818.6	43	40	17	1.8	1.2
Allstate Ins. Co.	5156.0	67	8054.9	54	32	14	1.0	2.2
Hartford Acc. & Indemnity Co.	1044.6	27	2458.9	79	16	5	1.6	1.7
Averages	2096.6	38	4222.5	60	22	19	1.4	2.1
The *Value Line* Companies:								
Chubb Corp.	1002.9	n.a.	2745.5	45	18	37	n.a.	n.a.
Continental Corp.	2428.6	32	8216.0	32	25	43	n.a.	n.a.
Crum and Forster	1660.6	21	3896.2	54	16	30	1.5	2.4
GEICO Corp.	653.1	90	1474.6	48	18	34	1.5	4.8
INA Corp.	2998.0	n.a.	10603.7	51	8	41	2.2	2.2
Mission Ins. Grp. Inc.	n.a.	n.a.	775.4	63	8	29	n.a.	n.a.
Ohio Casualty Corp.	800.2	49	1387.0	65	15	20	1.0	2.1
Safeco Corp.	820.2	45	2623.9	39	18	44	1.1	1.3
St. Paul Companies	1520.1	20	4252.4	58	14	28	1.6	1.7
U.S. Fid. & Guar. Co.	2043.7	33	4247.3	55	23	22	1.2	2.5
Averages	1547.5	41	4022.2	49	17	34	1.6	2.3

distribution of the underwriting portfolio and firm risk as measured by β_E.

In general, possible alternatives to the Fairley model for setting profit rates should be kept in mind when assessing the efficacy of using the *Value Line* figures. The traditional fixed profit margin method necessarily assumed similar risk across many types of insurance and states. Another alternative, the use of a target return to equity equal to the average return for all industries provides no basis for distinguishing the risk of one type of insurance firm from that of another. Consequently, while use of the Fairley method and the *Value Line* sample involves some a priori assumptions about the comparability of firms, the assumptions are less strong than those underlying the alternative methods.

The Basic Parameters. The estimated parameters for the seven-firm sample from 1967 to 1980, and the ten-firm sample from 1972 to 1980 are presented in table 2-3.[12] Both samples include Government Employees Insurance Company (GEICO), which Fairley omitted. Calculations were repeated without GEICO and the results did not change significantly. The beta of assets, β_A, is calculated according to the formula Fairley used, $\beta_A = SW \times \beta_S + BW \times \beta_B$, where β_S and β_B are the betas of stocks and bonds, respectively, and SW and BW are stock and bond weights.[13] The stock and bond weights were calculated using the expanded sample. The betas for stocks and bonds are those used in the original Fairley paper: $\beta_S = 1.0$ and $\beta_B = 0.125$. The tax rate on underwriting, $t = 0.24$, and the tax rate on assets, $t_a = 0.21$, are the results of the linear regression of total

Table 2-3. Parameter Estimates for the Seven- and Ten-Firm Samples

	Seven-Firm Sample				*Ten-Firm Sample*	
Parameter[a]	*1967–1971*	*1971–1975*	*1972–1976*	*1976–1980*	*1972–1976*	*1976–1980*
s	1.00	1.24	1.42	1.93	1.33	1.85
k	0.78	0.72	0.76	1.10	0.74	1.09
k_N	0.68	0.77	0.77	0.85	0.82	0.88
β_A	0.63	0.52	0.48	0.34	0.47	0.34
t	0.24	0.24	0.24	0.24	0.24	0.24
t_a	0.21	0.21	0.21	0.21	0.21	0.21
β_E	0.87	0.98	1.00	1.03	1.00	1.03
$\beta_L(\beta_N{=}0)$	0.01	−0.14	−0.13	−0.06	−0.17	−0.08
$\beta_L(\beta_N{=}0.125)$	0.08	−0.08	−0.06	0.01	−0.10	−0.02

[a] See the text for descriptions of the parameters and the sample.

taxes paid on underwriting and investment income described earlier.

Value Line calculates the beta of equity based on five years of monthly returns. This explains the division of the sample into five-year periods. For the ten-firm sample, 1972–1976 is the earliest period available. Fairley's original estimates were based on 1971–1975. The reported β_E in the tables is a weighted average of the betas of each company, where the value of equity determines the weights. In contrast to Fairley's original work, market rather than book data always were used to measure the value of equity.

The Beta of Liabilities. The beta of liabilities, β_L, is the principal variable of interest in table 2-3. Two estimates are reported, one with the beta of nontraded assets assumed to be zero and one where it is assumed to be 0.125.

In both samples, the estimates of β_L generally are negative and very close to zero. (A negative β_L implies positive underwriting risk.) Also, under either assumption about the value of β_N, the variation in β_L over the sample period is small. For example, in the seven-firm sample when $\beta_N = 0$, all β_L values lie between -0.15 and 0.02. Increasing the value of β_N from 0 to 0.125 slightly increases the estimated β_L, as was predicted by equation (2.13). Furthermore, the magnitude of this increase, roughly 0.07, is the same in both samples and all time periods.

Using the average value of k for Massachusetts firms, a change in the estimate of β_L of 0.1 results in less than a one percentage point change in the profit rate. Hence, from a practical standpoint, the estimates of β_L reported in table 2-3 change little through time and across samples. Note that this stability holds in spite of the relatively large changes over time in both the premium-to-surplus ratio (s) and the beta of traded assets (β_A).[14]

The results shown in table 2-3 tend to support Fairley's original finding that the beta of liabilities is a small negative number. In addition to these results, estimates of β_L were calculated for all five-year periods between 1967 and 1980 for the seven-firm sample and between 1972 and 1980 for the ten-firm sample. The estimate with the largest absolute value was -0.22. Since Fairley's estimate of β_L was -0.21, his corresponding estimate of β_p might be considered an upper bound on the systematic risk of the underwriting profit rate.

Illustrative Profit Rate Calculations

This section presents some calculations that are designed to illustrate the profit rates implied by the suggested revisions of the Fairley model. The profit rate depends critically on the value chosen for the risk-free rate of interest. For illustrative purposes, yields available on an arbitrarily selected recent day were used. The authors do not necessarily suggest that these yields would be appropriate for actual rate setting. Massachusetts data were used for the timing of the cash flow. The convenient approximations that premiums were received at the beginning of the year and all losses were paid on a single date also were used in the calculations.

The specific formula used to estimate the equilibrium profit rates by line of insurance is a two-tax rate version of the original Fairley formula:

$$p_N = \frac{r_f t_a}{(1 - t)s} - \frac{r_f(1 - t_a)k}{1 - t} - ck\beta_L(r_m - r_f) \tag{2.15}$$

where c is a modified version of Fairley's "conversion factor."[15] The parameter values used to estimate p_N are presented in table 2-4.

The data contained in table 2-4 were generally derived from the experience of Massachusetts firms. One exception is the premium-to-surplus ratio of 2.0 which is a standard benchmark. Also, Fairley's original beta for liabilities of −0.21 is used. As noted earlier, this figure is probably a lower bound for β_L and, as a result, provides an upper bound for that portion of the profit formula that supplies a risk premium for underwriting. The risk premium $(r_m - r_f)$ is the average during 1926–1980 of the difference between the return on the Standard and Poors 500 Index and the Treasury bill rate.[16]

The risk-free interest rate used in the profit rate calculations is the

Table 2-4. Parameter Values for the Illustrative Profit Rate Calculations for Auto Insurance

Parameter[a]	*Bodily Injury*	*Property Damage*	*Overall*
s	2.00	2.00	2.00
k	1.51	0.38	0.99
β_L	−0.21	−0.21	−0.21
β_A	0.36	0.36	0.36
t	0.46	0.46	0.46
t_a	0.28	0.28	0.28
c	0.91	1.11	1.00
$(r_m - r_f)$	0.09	0.09	0.09
r_f	0.1644	0.1711	0.1675

[a] See the text for descriptions of the parameters.

Treasury bill rate for bonds with a maturity roughly equal to the length of the cash flow for each line, as reported in the *Wall Street Journal*, August 15, 1981. For example, r_f for bodily injury is the rate for an 18-month Treasury bond, interpolated from the one- and two-year rates. The tax rate on assets has been estimated using equation (2.4) where the portfolio weights of Massachusetts firms are from data compiled by the Massachusetts State Rating Bureau in the 1982 commercial automobile rate hearings (see Commonwealth of Massachusetts, 1981, exhibit 6B). The figure used for t_a (0.28) is higher than the Bureau's (0.22) because it was adjusted to reflect the implicit tax paid by insurance companies through the lower yield on tax-exempt securities. Specifically, the Bureau's figure is taxes paid per dollar of investment income. This number was increased by the margin in rates between long-term government bonds and municipal bonds times the weight of tax-exempts in total investment income. This correction is required in order to be consistent with the assumption of the Fairley model that the expected pretax return on investments is the CAPM equilibrium return.[17]

Two sets of profit rates and associated returns to equity are shown in table 2-5. One set assumes the firm has some taxable income so that underwriting losses provide a (marginal) tax shield at a rate of 46 percent. [See equation (2.3).] The second case assumes that underwriting losses exceed all taxable investment income. [See equation (2.5).] A firm that does business only in Massachusetts and writes only automobile insurance would pay no taxes given the profit rates shown in table 2-5.

The returns to equity are higher in the no-tax case. The reason is that the firm becomes riskier when the U.S. Treasury is no longer a "partner" in the enterprise. The tax assumption affects profit rates differently for the two lines. The bodily injury profit rate is higher in the no-tax case than in the tax case because underwriting losses are relatively large compared to investment income. As a result, the value of the losses as a tax shield exceeds the tax liabilities incurred due to investment income. Net income falls when one assumes no taxes are paid, and the profit rate must rise to compensate. For property damage the reverse is true. Taxes on investment income exceed the value of the tax shield from underwriting losses. Hence, in the no-tax regime income rises and the profit rate must fall to compensate.

The magnitude of the negative profit rates may appear to be unreasonably large, especially for bodily injury and both lines combined, but they nevertheless produce reasonable returns to equity.[18] The large magnitudes reflect the long claims tail for bodily injury and high interest rates. When Treasury bill yields are in the neighborhood of 17 percent, every 79¢ of

Table 2-5. Illustrative Profit Rates and Returns to Equity

Tax Rates	*Line*	*Profit Rate* (p_N)[a]	*Return to Equity* (r_e)[b]
$t_a = 0.28, t = 0.46$	Bodily injury	−26.2%	28.6%
	Property damage	−3.4	22.1
	Overall	−15.9	25.7
$t_a = t = 0$	Bodily injury	−22.2%	34.7%
	Property damage	−5.7	24.4
	Overall	−14.7	30.1

[a] Profit rates are calculated using equation (2.15) with the given tax rates and the remaining parameter values shown in table 2-4.

[b] Returns to equity are calculated from $r_e = (ks + 1)(1 - t_a)[r_f + \beta_A(r_m - r_f)] + p_N s(1 - t)$.

premiums grows to $1 by the time the average bodily injury claim is paid. Since two dollars of premiums are assumed to be written for each dollar of equity, investment income is able to offset the large underwriting "losses" and yield sizable returns to equity.

The Profit Rate and Inflation

The underwriting profit margin given by equation (2.15) depends on the nominal rate of interest. Since t_a/s generally will be substantially smaller than $(1 - t_a)k$ and interest rates tend to rise with inflation, the profit margin will tend to decline with inflation. This relationship contributes to the large negative profit rates in table 2-5.

The rise in interest rates under inflation does not represent a rise in real returns but rather provides compensation for the erosion of purchasing power. The question arises as to whether use of the nominal risk-free rate in equation (2.15) is appropriate, as opposed to using an estimate of the real rate of return available on Treasury bills. The use of a real rate would substantially influence the results during periods of high inflation. However, the discussion that follows indicates that the use of nominal rates is justified.

Consider the underwriting margin, γ, defined as the excess of premiums over losses at prices prevailing at the time the contracts are sold and premiums are paid as a proportion of losses, i.e.,

$$\gamma = \frac{P - Z}{Z} \tag{2.16}$$

where P denotes premiums and Z denotes losses. It will be shown for some simple situations that the expected value of γ obtained by using p_N from equation (2.15) depends only on the real rate of interest and not on the inflation rate, provided that the estimate of expected losses used to calculate premiums contains an allowance for expected future inflation in losses. In other words, the use of equation (2.15) with a nominal value of r_f and expected losses appropriately defined will tend to insure that the relationship between premiums and losses at current prices is unaffected by inflation so that no modification in equation (2.15) is needed.

The variability of actual losses can be decomposed into two parts. First, let ε be the proportionate variation in claims around their expected value measured in constant dollars—that is, around the expected value of Z. The component ε represents errors in forecasting the number of claims and their severity while holding all prices constant. This will be called the "real" component of risk. Second, let q be the (average) rate of inflation between the time the premium is paid and the time the claim is settled. Note that q, a random variable, is not necessarily the general rate of inflation in the economy. If medical or repair costs rise more rapidly than, say, the CPI, then a rise in q will reflect a rise in real claim costs to some extent. Nevertheless, for simplicity, q will be called the "inflation" component of risk.

Letting a bar over a variable denote expected value, actual loss payments are

$$L = \bar{Z}(1 + kq)(1 + \varepsilon) \tag{2.17}$$

where k, as before, is the average period of the cash flow. Let $\bar{p}$ denote the expected value of the traditional underwriting profit margin, ignoring transaction costs—that is, $\bar{p} = (P - \bar{L})/P$. Then the expected value of γ as defined in equation (2.16) can be expressed as[19]

$$\bar{\gamma} = \frac{p + k\bar{q}}{1 - \bar{p}} \tag{2.18}$$

Assume that premiums are set equal to the expected value of nominal losses plus the profit margin given by $\bar{p}$—that is, $P = \bar{L} + \bar{p}P$. Solving for P and substituting from equations (2.17) and (2.18) gives

$$P = \bar{Z}(1 + \bar{\gamma}) \tag{2.19}$$

For notational convenience, let a new "turnover" ratio be defined as:

$$s^* = Z/V_E = \frac{s}{(1 + \gamma)} \tag{2.20}$$

Using equations (2.17), (2.19), and (2.20), the realized return on equity is given by

$$r_E = (ks + 1)r_a(1 - t_a) + \frac{[(1 + \bar{\gamma})\bar{Z} - \bar{Z}(1 + kq)(1 + \varepsilon)](1 - t)}{V_E}$$

$$= (ks + 1)r_a(1 - t_a) + s^*[(\bar{\gamma} - kq) - (1 + kq)\varepsilon](1 - t) \qquad (2.21)$$

The beta of equity is:

$$\beta_E = (ks + 1)(1 - t_a)\beta_A - s^*[k\beta_q + \beta_\varepsilon + k\beta_{q\varepsilon}](1 - t) \qquad (2.22)$$

Neglecting the term $k\beta_{q\varepsilon}$ gives

$$\beta_E = (ks + 1)(1 - t_a)\beta_A - s^*(k\beta_q + \beta_\varepsilon)(1 - t) \qquad (2.23)$$

Let $\Pi = (\bar{r}_m - r_f)$ in the CAPM equation for equilibrium returns. Equating the CAPM equilibrium (r_E^g) and expected ($\bar{r}_E$) returns to equity yields

$$r_E^g = r_f + \beta_E\Pi = (ks + 1)(1 - t_a)r_a + s^*(\bar{\gamma} - k\bar{q})(1 - t) = \bar{r}_E$$

since $\bar{\varepsilon}$ equals zero. Substituting for β_E gives

$$r_f + [(ks + 1)(1 - t_a)\beta_A - s^*(k\beta_q + \beta_\varepsilon)(1 - t)\Pi$$
$$= (ks + 1)(1 - t_a)r_a + s^*(\bar{\gamma} - k\bar{q})(1 - t)$$

Since $r_a = r_f + \beta_A\Pi$ and $s = s^*(1 + \bar{\gamma})$, this reduces to

$$\bar{\gamma} = \frac{\dfrac{r_f t_a}{s^*(1 - t)} - kr_f\dfrac{(1 - t_a)}{(1 - t)} - (k\beta_q + \beta_\varepsilon)\Pi + k\bar{q}}{1 + r_f k\dfrac{(1 - t_a)}{(1 - t)}} \qquad (2.24)$$

The denominator of equation (2.24) is a number close to unity. Hence, comparing equations (2.15) and (2.24), it can be seen that the expected real profit rate is approximately equal to the traditional profit rate, p, plus an allowance for expected inflation, $k\bar{q}$. The term $(k\beta_q + \beta_\varepsilon)\Pi$ has replaced the risk premium in the Fairley model.[20] Note that only the inflation component of the risk premium is proportional to the lag in claim payments given by k. The term β_ε, which is the risk due to errors in forecasting accident frequency or severity, is not multiplied by k. This makes sense intuitively since the events that give rise to these errors all take place within the fixed time period covered by the policy (i.e., one year). The fact that claim payments extend beyond the end of the policy year does not affect the incidence of accidents within that year. On the other hand, errors in predicting the cost of a claim (of given severity) are proportional to the lag in payment. If there is an error in predicting the general level of inflation or some particular component of cost, the magnitude of the error increases over time.

The implication of this result is that in order to set profit margins by line, given some overall assessment of the risk of underwriting, the relative magnitudes of both sources of risk must be known. In principle, the systematic risk of the real component can be estimated by comparing actual accident frequency and severity with those assumed when the rates are set by the ISO or some other rating organization. However, such data are not now available over a sufficient period for reasonable estimation. In the absence of other information, the analysis suggests only that there is some basis for assuming longer-tailed lines have greater risk, but the exact nature of the relationship cannot be determined a priori.

Another implication of equation (2.24) is that, in the absence of taxes, the real risk premium is roughly independent of inflation. With $t = t_a = 0$, equation (2.24) can be rewritten as

$$\bar{\gamma} = -(k\beta_q + \beta_\varepsilon)\Pi - k(r_f - \bar{q}) \tag{2.25}$$

The second term, $(r_f - \bar{q})$, is approximately equal to the real rate of interest so that neither term will be significantly influenced by claims inflation, provided that $\bar{q}$ is approximately equal to the overall rate of inflation in the economy. If so, a rise in expected inflation in claim costs is offset by a corresponding increase in the ability to earn higher nominal yields on investments. As a result, the expected real profit margin produced by the Fairley model is largely independent of inflation, except to the extent that taxes on nominal yields must be accounted for. Of course, the actual rate of inflation may differ from its expected value, but that possibility is reflected in the risk premium, $k\beta_q$.

This result also can be interpreted in terms of the traditional profit rate, p. This rate, measured relative to claims expressed in actual dollars paid out, is inversely related to expected inflation. When expected inflation rises, so do interest rates. In order to maintain a constant real profit margin, p must fall to offset the increased ability to earn investment income.

Note that the insensitivity of the real profit rate to inflation depends critically on the assumption that the estimate of expected loss payments, $\bar{L}$ (including expected expenses as well), accounts for expected inflation over the period in which claims are paid. This assumption accurately reflects regulatory intention. However, it is common actuarial practice to forecast variables by extending historical trends. Most investors seem to have consistently underestimated the rise in inflation over the past two decades. Extrapolating past trends probably gave downward-biased estimates. (If inflation now begins to fall, there will, of course, be an upward bias in such estimates.) This problem illustrates the general principle that profit regulation of any kind can only be efficacious when costs are realistically estimated.

Concluding Comments

There are two principal advantages of the Fairley model relative to alternative procedures for setting underwriting profit margins in nonlife insurance. First, the model relies on current yields available to investors. This ensures that at all times investors receive returns that are just adequate to attract the required equity capital into the industry. It also ensures that each year's policyholders are paying premiums that reflect investment income available during the policy year rather than investment income that was available to policyholders in previous years.

The second advantage is that at this time the Fairley model is the only one that provides a quantifiable measure of underwriting risk. The alternatives rely on subjective judgments of risk, with the result that there are clear incentives to shade one's opinion depending on the side one represents in a regulatory hearing. The Fairley model is less subjective since the derivation of its measure of risk is explicit. Its parameters can be tested, unlike a model that uses an a priori assumption about risk.

Of course, the Fairley model's measure of risk might be criticized because it is based on the Capital Asset Pricing Model. Over time the CAPM has been faulted on a number of grounds, and several alternative models of market equilibrium have been developed. However, even the creator of one of those alternative models acknowledges that

> . . . the attractiveness of the CAPM is due to its potential testability. It is a paradigm, precisely because it is cast in terms of variables which are, at least in principle and with the usual exception of the *ex ante ex post* distinction, empirically observable and statistically testable. Its positive orientation and apparently simple intuition have made it the central equilibrium model of financial economics. . . . (Ross 1978, p. 885)

Notes

1. In the CAPM, risk is determined by an asset's beta, defined as

$$\beta_i = \text{cov}(r_i, r_m)/[\text{var}(r_m)]$$

where r_i and r_m are the returns on asset i and the market portfolio of risky assets, respectively.

In practice, returns on a broad portfolio of common stocks generally are used for r_m.

2. The variation in risk among firms is one reason the traditional method of setting a return to equity should not be used in regulatory proceedings.

3. Treasury bills are free from default risk. The risk of capital losses also is minimal because of their short maturity.

4. This point is developed more fully later in the chapter.

5. The rationale for assuming that 61 percent of capital gains are taxed at the 0.46 rate is that 0.61 times 0.46 gives the current capital gains rate of 0.28.

6. Note that $\Sigma_j w_j > 1.0$, since stocks produce both dividends and capital gains.

7. More formally, it is obvious from equation (2.2) that $dT/d(ps)$ equals t or minus t for p greater than zero or p less than zero, respectively, where ps is underwriting income per dollar of equity.

8. This estimated upper limit is based on an estimate of realized capital gains on stocks of 10 percent. Realized capital gains are likely to be significantly smaller for most firms.

9. For statutory annual statement and tax purposes, firms report premiums earned less incurred losses and expenses. Expenses, however, are roughly contemporaneous with premiums written. When premium income is growing, earned premiums are less than written premiums so that the statutory procedure understates GAAP underwriting income because of the failure to match revenues and expenses.

10. The estimates were obtained using Zellner's seemingly unrelated regression procedure (see Theil 1971, p. 297) and restricting the coefficients to be constant across firms. Both $\hat{\alpha}_1$ and $\hat{\alpha}_2$ were highly significant.

11. The values shown in table 2-2 for both groups were obtained from *Moody's* whenever possible to ensure consistency in the balance sheet data.

12. The ten-firm sample includes all of the *Value Line* companies shown in table 2-2. The seven-firm sample omits Chubb, Mission, and SAFECO due to the lack of equity betas for these firms until the later period.

13. Specifically, SW equals $S/(S + B)$ and BW equals $B/(S + B)$ where S and B equal the values of stocks and bonds, respectively.

14. The changes in β_A are caused by changes in the stock-bond mix of the firms only, since stock and bond betas were assumed to be constant over all of the periods analyzed.

15. Equation (2.15) essentially was derived by equating the expected after-tax return on equity using equations (2.3) and (2.4) with the CAPM equilibrium expected return. A description of the conversion factor, which has only a minor influence on p_N, is available in an unpublished appendix to this paper. Its purpose is to adjust for the fact that insurer cash inflows and outflows are not one year apart, as is assumed in the derivation of the Fairley model.

16. The values reported in Ibbotsen and Sinquefield (1976), which have been updated through 1980, were used.

17. Suppose that taxable and tax-exempt bonds have the same beta, say β_b. The Fairley model assumes the expected return on both is $r_b = r_f + \beta_b(r_m - r_f)$. However, the return on tax-exempt bonds will be less than that for taxables by the amount of the implicit tax. Including the implicit tax in t_a produces a value of p_N using equation (2.15) that will compensate shareholders for the return foregone by holding tax exempts.

18. As shown in table 2-3, the average equity beta for firms in the *Value Line* sample was about one. With $r_m - r_f$ equal to 9 percent and r_f equal to 17 percent, the expected return on a firm's stock with a beta of one would be 26 percent.

19. Equation (2.18) actually gives the probability limit of γ.

20. Equation (2.24) also ignores the conversion factor.

References

Commonwealth of Massachusetts, Division of Insurance. 1981. *Hearings—1982 Commercial Automobile Rates*.

Fairley, W. 1979. Investment income and profit margins in property-liability insurance: Theory and empirical results. *Bell Journal of Economics* 10(Spring): 192–210.

Hamada, R. 1972. The effect of the firm's capital structure on the systematic risk of common stocks. *Journal of Finance* 27(May):435–455.

Hill, R. 1979. Profit regulation in property-liability insurance. *Bell Journal of Economics* 10(Spring):172–191.

Ibbotsen, R. and S. Sinquefield. 1976. Stocks, bonds, bills, and inflation: Year by year historical returns (1926–1974). *Journal of Business* 49(January):11–47.

Moody's Bank and Finance Manual. New York: Moody's Investors Service, Inc.

Munch, P., and D. Smallwood. 1978. Solvency regulation in the property-casualty insurance industry. Santa Monica, CA: Rand Corporation.

Rosenberg, B., and J. Guy. 1976a. "Prediction of beta from investment fundamentals: Part I." *Financial Analysts Journal* 32(May–June): 60–72.

Rosenberg, B., and J. Guy. 1976b. Prediction of beta from investment fundamentals: Part II. *Financial Analysts Journal* 32(July–August):62–70.

Ross, S. 1978. The current status of the capital asset pricing model. *Journal of Finance* 33(June):885–901.

Theil, H. 1971. *Principles of Econometrics*. New York: Wiley.

Value Line Investment Survey. New York: Value Line Inc.

Appendix 2A: The Level of Underwriting Losses Which Offsets Taxable Investment Income

As was discussed in the text, the marginal tax rate on underwriting income is the corporate tax rate as long as there is positive taxable income from investments and underwriting combined. In this appendix, an estimate of the underwriting profit rate at which the typical Massachusetts firm has no taxable income is derived. This profit rate produces underwriting losses that just equal taxable investment income.

Data developed by the Massachusetts State Rating Bureau for the 1982 commercial auto rate hearings (see Commonwealth of Massachusetts, 1981, exhibit 6B) give the portfolio weights and yields on investments shown below.

Category	*Portfolio Weight (w_j)*	*Yield*	*Proportion Taxable (v_j)*
Taxable bonds	0.268	0.0939	1.00
Tax-exempt bonds	0.486	0.0633	0.00
Dividends	0.222	0.0610	0.15
Capital gains	0.222	0.1070	1.00
Other assets	0.024	0.2174	1.00

In the text, the proportion of capital gains subject to tax was assumed to be 0.61 for notational convenience. The actual proportion taxable (1.0) is shown above.

Taxable investment income as a proportion of assets equals $\Sigma w_j v_j r_j =$ 5.62 percent. The weighted reserve-to-premium ratio is approximately 1.0 for bodily injury and property damage combined. With a premium-to-surplus ratio of 2.0, this implies that the ratio of assets to surplus $(ks + 1)$ is 3.0. Taxable investment income per dollar of surplus is therefore 3.0 × 5.62 percent = 16.86 percent. The cut-off profit ratio occurs where $-ps =$ 16.86 percent, or, for $s = 2.0$, at $p = -8.43$ percent.

Appendix 2B: The Effect of Assuming a 46 Percent Tax Rate for Investment Income

If $t_a = 0.46$ is used in equation (2.15) with the parameter values shown in table 2.4 to calculate the fair profit rate rather than $t_a = 0.28$, the profit rates and associated returns to equity increase substantially as is shown below. The profit rates and returns to equity for the $t_a = 0.28$ case are those shown in text table 2-5. The returns to equity for the $t_a = 0.46$ case assume that the profit rate is calculated using $t_a = 0.46$ but that actual investment income will be taxed at a 28 percent rate.

	Profit Rates		*Returns to Equity*	
Line	$t_a = 0.28$	$t_a = 0.46$	$t_a = 0.28$	$t_a = 0.46$
Bodily injury	−26.2%	−15.2%	28.6%	40.5%
Property damage	−3.4	1.6	22.1	27.5
Overall	−15.9	−7.6	25.7	34.7

3 A DISCOUNTED CASH FLOW APPROACH TO PROPERTY-LIABILITY INSURANCE RATE REGULATION

Stewart C. Myers and Richard A. Cohn

This chapter begins by considering how a fair system of rate regulation—fair to both policyholders and insurance-company stockholders—would work. This question is usually answered by defining a fair rate of return. However, fairness can be more clearly and generally defined in terms of present value.

Consider a property-liability insurance company in terms of an idealized balance sheet, shown in table 3-1. On the asset side, if we ignore the company's modest holdings of physical assets, are financial assets, primarily stocks and bonds. On the liability side, ignoring liabilities

---

Editor's note: This chapter is based on a paper prepared for the 1982 Massachusetts automobile rate hearings (Myers and Cohn 1981). The paper has been slightly modified for clarity and for consistency in notation. The Myers-Cohn paper introduced a discounted cash flow approach to insurance rate regulation and also criticized the procedures discussed in chapter 1, which describes the Massachusetts fair-rate-of-return procedures used in 1981. It was written at approximately the same time as chapter 2, which responds to some of the criticisms. The authors wish to thank Acheson H. Callaghan, Jr. and Richard Derrig for their help and advice.

Table 3-1. An Idealized Balance Sheet for a Property-Liability Insurance Company (market values)

Financial assets	Policy reserves (present value of expected losses and loss expenses)
	Equity value
Total value	Total value

Table 3-2. An Idealized Balance Sheet Recognizing Tax Liabilities (market values)

Financial assets	Policy reserves
	Present value of tax liability
	Equity value
Total value	Total value

unrelated to outstanding policies, are insurance-policy reserves and common equity. The policy reserves can be viewed as the present value of expected losses and expenses.[1]

A similar balance sheet exists for every policy the firm writes. The firm receives the premium, commits a portion of its stockholders' equity, and invests the total in securities. The policyholder's claim against these financial assets is recognized in policy reserves—i.e., the present value of expected losses and loss expenses. The equity claim represents the stockholders' investment plus the present value of expected underwriting profits. (Note that these balance-sheet items are defined as market or present values. The corresponding book values would be different.)

There are actually three sets of claimants to the company's financial assets: policyholders, who are entitled to benefits in the event of loss; shareholders, the residual owners; and various taxing authorities. The market or present values of these three sets of claims sum to the market value of the company's financial assets. A modified balance sheet showing the three sets of claims is presented in table 3-2.

Fair Regulation

The following definition of fairness is proposed: rate regulation should ensure that, whenever a policy is issued, the resulting equity value equals the equity invested in support of that policy.

A rate that led to a higher equity value would be unfair to the policyholder, for it would imply a wealth transfer from the policyholder to the shareholder. A rate that led to a lower equity value also would be unfair, for it would imply a wealth transfer from the shareholder to the policyholder.

A fair system of regulation is one in which the stockholders get what they pay for, no more and no less. Fair compensation to equity capital implies that the company is indifferent to whether or not an insurance policy is written. Premium income is invested in financial assets, and these assets and the income they produce are, on average, sufficient to pay losses, expenses, taxes, and a fair return to the shareholder for the risk that he or she bears.

It follows that the allowed premium, if rates are to be fair, should be set equal to the sum of (1) the present value of losses and expenses and (2) the present value of the tax burden on the insurer's underwriting and investment income. Note that the financial assets supporting a policy equal the policy premium plus the equity invested in support of the policy. As table 3-3 shows, if the premium covers the present values of expected losses, expenses, and taxes, then equity value equals equity investment.[2] In other words, investors are given the prospect of a fair return—a return that will, on average, compensate them for "loaning out" their money to back up the policy, for bearing risk, and for the tax payments generated by the policy.

It is fair for the policyholders to pay the tax on investment income, even though some of the invested capital is provided by the shareholders, because shareholders can invest on their own in stocks and bonds. They would not willingly invest in a corporation that bought marketable securities if their investment income was thereby subjected to an additional

Table 3-3. Balance Sheet for Fairly-Priced Insurance Policy (market values at start of policy)

Financial assets reflecting:	
Premium received	{ Present value of losses and loss expenses Present value of tax liability
Equity investment	Equity value
Total value	Total value

layer of taxation. Therefore, the policyholders should bear the tax penalties associated with the corporate form of insurance enterprise.

A set of discount rates is needed to calculate the present values of losses, expenses and taxes. In the analysis that follows, the capital-asset pricing model (CAPM) is used to calculate the required discount rates. What matters for rate-setting purposes is present value; the CAPM is used to obtain these values in part because it has been employed in Massachusetts. The present value or discounted cash flow approach does not depend on the CAPM, however.

The Fairley Formula

William Fairley (1979) has developed a formula based on the CAPM for calculating a fair premium rate. However, that formula is inconsistent with present-value analysis.

Fairley's formula was developed by making a series of arbitrary assumptions and approximations. These approximations were justified as reasonable simplifications. Fairley's procedure, however, turns out to be a complicated approximation to a very simple truth. Rate-of-return regulation of insurance premiums requires only two simple steps. The allowed premium should be set equal to the sum of (1) the present value of expenses and payments to policyholders and (2) the present value of the tax burden on the insurance company's investment and underwriting income. The Fairiey formula does not give the same allowed premiums as this simple two-step procedure.

Example

A simple example is used to illustrate the difference between the present-value method and Fairley's formula. The appendix to this chapter contains a formal statement of the two procedures and more realistic numerical examples.

Consider a group of policies on which the entire premium P is paid in advance and received today (at period 0). All losses and expenses are paid out one period hence (at period 1). Expected losses and expenses are denoted by L. The problem is to determine the fair level for P as a fraction of L. P should equal the present value of L plus the present value of taxes on underwriting and investment income.

The present value of L is found by discounting at r_L, an appropriate risk-adjusted discount rate.

$$PV(L) = \frac{L}{1 + r_L} \tag{3.1}$$

where $PV(L)$ = present value of L. The discount rate r_L can be calculated from the CAPM formula:

$$r_L = r_f + \beta_L(r_m - r_f) \tag{3.2}$$

where

r_f = the one-period risk-free interest rate
β_L = $\text{cov}(\tilde{r}_L, \tilde{r}_m)/\text{var}(\tilde{r}_m)$, the beta of the uncertain losses $\tilde{L}$ (tildes are used to distinguish random variables from their expectations)
r_m = the expected rate of return on the market portfolio

In this example, let $r_f = 0.10$, $r_m = 0.19$, and $\beta_L = -0.2$. Then, $r_L = 0.10 - 0.2(0.19 - 0.10) = 0.082$, and

$$PV(L) = \frac{L}{1.082} = 0.9242L$$

The firm will also have to pay taxes in period 1 on its underwriting profit. Assume that the tax rate is $\tau = 0.40$. The tax will be $0.4P - 0.4L$. To obtain the present value of this underwriting tax, discount $0.4P$ at r_f (since P is received in period 0 and known with certainty) and $0.4L$ at r_L.

$$PV(UWPT) = \frac{0.4P}{1.1} - \frac{0.4L}{1.082} = 0.3636P - 0.3697L$$

where $PV(UWPT)$ = the present value of $UWPT$, the tax on underwriting income.

Now calculate the tax on investment income. Assume that the firm invests P plus an equal amount of its surplus in risk-free securities. (That is, the surplus backing the policy is assumed to be equal to P.) It will earn interest income of $r_f(2P)$ and pay a tax of $\tau r_f(2P)$. The present value of this tax is[3]

$$PV(IBT) = \frac{\tau r_f(2P)}{1 + r_f} = \frac{0.4(0.10)2P}{1.1} = 0.0727P$$

where $PV(IBT)$ = the present value of IBT the tax on investment income. Here we assume the tax rates for underwriting and investment income are the same.

The final step is to solve for the fair value of P:

$$P = PV(L) + PV(UWPT) + PV(IBT)$$

$$= 0.9242L + 0.3636P - 0.3697L + 0.0727P$$

$$= 0.9837L \tag{3.3}$$

Fairley's formula gives $P = 0.9914L$, approximately a percentage point higher (see the appendix to this chapter).

Simulations

It proved impossible to find any tractable algebraic formula to predict the errors resulting from use of the Fairley formula. Instead, the authors wrote a simple computer program to calculate fair values of P using both the discounted cash flow and Fairley methods. Base-case numerical examples were constructed for automobile bodily-injury and liability property-damage insurance, respectively. Time patterns for premiums and losses were based on actual patterns used by the Massachusetts Division of Insurance in setting automobile insurance rates. The time patterns are shown in table 3-4.

The results of the simulations are presented in tables 3-5 and 3-6. The fair premiums for the base case are in bold face. The premiums are expressed as percentages of expected losses and expenses (e.g., a table entry of 95 would imply that the fair premium is 95 percent of expected losses and expenses). The parameters for the base case are similar to those used in the example given above.

The base-case results for bodily-injury liability insurance (table 3-5) reveal that the premium based on Fairley's formula is 4.9 percentage points less than that based on the discounted cash flow method. For property-damage insurance (table 3-6), the Fairley formula yields a premium that is 0.7 percentage points too high. The accuracy of the Fairley formula is sensitive not only to the time patterns of premiums and losses but also to the values assumed for the risk-free rate of interest, r_f, the effective corporate tax rate, τ, the systematic risk of losses and loss expenses, β_L, and the amount of equity capital required as a proportion of P. The results of these calculations are also shown in table 3-5 and 3-6. For bodily-injury liability insurance, the differences ranged from 0.278 to 13.011 percentage points; for property-damage liability insurance they ranged from 0.397 to −2.464 percentage points. These are significant errors in an industry where a swing of plus or minus one or two percentage points in underwriting income can have a dramatic impact on net profits. Moreover, the errors are unnecessary; they reflect the various approximations Fairley employed in developing his roundabout procedure. The present-value

Table 3-4. Automobile Insurance Cash Flow Patterns[a]

	Bodily-Injury Liability		*Property-Damage*	
Quarter	*P(fraction)*	*L(fraction)*	*P(fraction)*	*L(fraction)*
0	0.0060	0.0238	0.0060	0.0222
1	0.5526	0.1331	0.5526	0.1681
2	0.3617	0.1047	0.3617	0.2251
3	0.0689	0.0747	0.0689	0.1977
4	0.0109	0.0750	0.0109	0.2218
5		0.0582		0.0999
6		0.0528		0.0189
7		0.0484		0.0144
8		0.0401		0.0178
9		0.0339		0.0049
10		0.0262		0.0035
11		0.0268		0.0021
12		0.0229		0.0022
13		0.0237		
14		0.0236		
15		0.0174		0.0013
16		0.0114		
19		0.0987		
23		0.0541		
27		0.0306		
31		0.0122		
35		0.0050		
39		0.0025		

[a] Table entries represent the cash flow pattern for a block of policies issued in quarter 0. The entries stand for the proportion of premiums and losses paid in each quarter. Columns do not add to 1.0, due to rounding.

Source: Massachusetts Division of Insurance, based on data available in 1981.

approach is simple and direct. It does not require approximations.

Other Conceptual Problems

The simulations just discussed show the errors introduced by the approximations Fairley employed. His procedure can also be questioned at a more basic level.

One example is the use of a single tax rate for both investment and

Table 3-5. Fair Premium Ratios for Automobile Bodily-Injury Liability Insurance[a] (percent)

	Discounted Cash Flow Method	*Fairley Formula*	*Difference*
	Effect of varying τ		
$\tau = 0$	87.867%	87.589%	0.278%
0.1	89.267	88.311	0.956
0.2	91.081	89.231	1.850
0.3	93.525	90.442	3.083
0.4	**96.995**	**92.109**	**4.886**
0.5	102.310	94.549	7.761
0.6	111.472	98.461	13.011
	Effect of varying β_L		
$\beta_L = -0.4$	100.040%	94.826%	5.214%
−0.3	98.492	93.448	5.044
−0.2	**96.995**	**92.109**	**4.886**
−0.1	95.548	90.796	4.752
0	94.146	89.507	4.639
0.1	92.790	88.254	4.536
0.2	91.476	87.025	4.451
0.3	90.203	85.818	4.385
0.4	88.970	84.644	4.326
	Effect of varying S		
$S = 1.0$	100.119%	93.557%	6.562%
1.1	98.865	92.981	5.884
1.2	97.843	92.507	5.336
1.3	**96.995**	**92.109**	**4.886**
1.4	96.280	91.771	4.503
1.5	95.669	91.479	4.190
2.0	93.589	90.475	3.114
2.5	92.384	89.882	2.502
3.0	91.598	89.492	2.106
3.5	91.045	89.215	1.830
4.0	90.634	89.008	1.626
	Effect of varying r_f		
$r_f = 0.012$	100.064%	97.059%	3.005%
0.020	97.961	93.711	4.250

Table 3-5. *(continued)*

	Discounted Cash Flow Method	*Fairley Formula*	*Difference*
0.023	97.232	92.538	4.694
0.024	**96.995**	**92.109**	**4.886**
0.025	96.762	91.763	4.999
0.030	95.647	90.013	5.694
0.035	94.609	88.437	6.172

[a] Table entries are ratios of fair premiums to expected losses, expressed as percentages. For example, 95 would indicate a premium equal to 95 percent of expected losses. Results for the *base case* are in bold face. The other entries were generated by varying the indicated parameters one at a time. The parameters for the *base case* are as follows: $r_f = 0.024$, $r_m - r_f = 0.0213$, $r_L = 0.0197$, $\beta_L = -0.2$, $\tau = \tau_\mu = \tau_r = 0.4$, $S = 1.3$, where r_f = the risk-free rate of interest per quarter, r_m = the expected return on the market portfolio per quarter, r_L = the risk-adjusted discount rate $r_f + \beta_L(r_m - r_f)$, $\beta_L = \text{cov}(\tilde{r}_L, \tilde{r}_m)/\text{var}(\tilde{r}_m)$, and S = the premium-to-surplus ratio. The cash flow patterns used in preparing this table are shown in table 3-4. The proportions assigned to quarters 17–20, 21–24, 25–28, 29–32, 33–36, and 37–40 have been apportioned uniformly across the appropriate four-quarter period. The discounting assumes that each quarter represents evaluation at the middle of the quarter.

Table 3-6. Fair Premium Ratios for Automobile Property-Damage Insurance[a] (percent)

	Present Value Method	*Fairley Formula*	*Difference*
	Effect of varying τ		
$\tau = 0$	97.410%	97.013%	0.397%
0.1	98.018	97.797	0.221
0.2	98.789	98.794	−0.005
0.3	99.799	100.107	−0.308
0.4	**101.177**	**101.913**	**−0.736**
0.5	103.172	104.553	−1.381
0.6	106.316	108.780	−2.464
	Effect of varying β_L		
$\beta_L = -0.4$	102.261%	102.620%	−0.359%
−0.3	101.716	102.265	−0.549
−0.2	**101.177**	**101.913**	**−0.736**
−0.1	100.643	101.560	−0.917

Table 3-6. *(continued)*

	Present Value Method	*Fairley Formula*	*Difference*
0	100.115	101.206	−1.091
0.1	99.592	100.854	−1.262
0.2	99.074	100.501	−1.427
0.3	98.561	100.148	−1.587
0.4	98.053	99.797	−1.744
	Effect of varying S		
S = 1.0	102.366%	103.481%	−1.115%
1.1	101.895	102.857	−0.962
1.2	101.505	102.344	−0.839
1.3	**101.177**	**101.913**	**−0.736**
1.4	100.898	101.547	−0.649
1.5	100.657	101.231	−0.574
2.0	99.824	100.143	−0.319
2.5	99.331	99.501	−0.170
3.0	99.004	99.077	−0.073
3.5	98.773	98.777	−0.004
4.0	98.600	98.553	0.047
	Effect of varying r_f		
r_f = 0.012	101.107%	101.264%	−0.157%
0.020	101.148	101.681	−0.533
0.023	101.169	101.848	−0.679
0.024	**101.177**	**101.913**	**−0.736**
0.025	101.185	101.963	−0.778
0.030	101.231	102.248	−1.017
0.035	101.287	102.536	−1.249

[a] Table entries are ratios of fair premiums to expected losses, expressed as percentages. For example, 95 would indicate a premium equal to 95 percent of expected losses. Results for the *base case* are in bold face. The other entries were generated by varying the indicated parameters one at a time. The parameters for the *base case* are as follows: $r_f = 0.024$, $r_m - r_f = 0.0213$, $r_L = 0.0197$, $\beta_L = -0.2$, $\tau = \tau_\mu = \tau_r = 0.4$, $S = 1.3$, where r_f = the risk-free rate of interest per quarter, r_m = the expected return on the market portfolio per quarter, r_L = the risk-adjusted discount rate $r_f + \beta_L(r_m - r_f)$, $\beta_L = \text{cov}(\tilde{r}_L, \tilde{r}_m)/\text{var}(\tilde{r}_m)$, and S = the premium-to-surplus ratio. The cash flow patterns used in preparing this table are shown in table 3-4. The proportions assigned to quarters 13–16 have been apportioned uniformly across that four-quarter period.

underwriting income. Actually, underwriting income should be taxed at a full marginal corporate tax rate. Investment income may be taxed at lower rates if investments are made in tax-exempt bonds, preferred stock, etc. Since the ratio of underwriting to investment income varies by policy type, the use of a single rate cannot give the correct premium for all policy types. Moreover, the low tax rate on investment income is usually achieved by accepting lower pretax yields. For example, dividends on preferred stocks are taxed at an effective rate of approximately 7 percent. However, this understates the full tax costs of investing in preferred stocks, because their tax advantages to corporate holders have driven yields below what insurance companies' shareholders could obtain on similarly risky bonds.

There is little in the insurance literature regarding the optimal asset portfolio, given taxes, for an insurance company. Are insurance companies' common-stock values reduced by the seeming tax disadvantage associated with corporate purchases of taxable marketable securities? Conversely, are they increased by the apparent tax advantage of borrowing? These questions are currently matters of great controversy in financial economics. The view taken in the present-value analysis used in this report (i.e., that common shares are reduced in value, other things equal, by the present value of the corporate tax liability resulting from purchases of taxable securities) is admittedly only one view.[4] The opposite view is that common-stock values are unaffected by the corporation's lending-borrowing decision even in the presence of taxes (Miller 1977).

The truth, as is usually the case when polar views clamor for attention, probably lies somewhere in between.[5] The problem is that experts currently do not know precisely where the truth lies. Consequently, the present-value approach as it is employed in this report, as well as the Fairley formula, are probably not exactly correct in specifying fair insurance premiums, and it is not clear just how the approach should be modified so as to take corporate taxes properly into account.

Problems of Measurement

Rate-of-return regulation in insurance involves calculating the present value of the costs and liabilities incurred when an insurance policy is written. This procedure requires a discount rate. If a discount rate is calculated from the CAPM, one must measure β_L, the beta of the insurance policy. But insurance policies are assets which are never traded directly in capital markets. Risk thus has to be inferred indirectly. The procedure used by the Massachusetts State Racing Bureau to estimate β_L

is not necessarily the best, but it illustrates the difficulties inevitably encountered. (The procedure is explained in chapters 1 and 2 of this book.) Some of the difficulties are discussed below:

1. The measurement of β_L depends upon estimated betas for insurance companies' securities portfolios. Information on the composition of these portfolios is available only sporadically. In any event, portfolio composition varies widely from company to company and over time. The estimates of investment-portfolio betas used by the Massachusetts Division of Insurance are clearly very rough.

2. The measurement of β_L also requires a measure of the beta of the common stock of the insurance companies themselves. Considerable random measurement error is routinely encountered in estimating betas for common stocks.

3. The measurement of β_L assumes that insurance companies have no assets but securities, and no liabilities except those resulting from the sale of policies. But several of the companies in the sample used by Fairley and the State Rating Bureau have invested outside of insurance. For example, Continental Corporation is involved in the credit-card business and INA Corporation in investment banking. Furthermore, even undiversified insurance companies may have intangible assets or contingent liabilities not shown on their balance sheets.

4. There is no reason to believe that β_L is the same for different lines of insurance, but the Massachusetts procedure is forced to adopt this assumption. The insurance companies for which β_L has been calculated concentrate in different lines. This may explain the differences in their betas; but since only a few companies can be analyzed, this hypothesis probably cannot be tested adequately.[6]

5. The implementation of the Fairley formula in Massachusetts can also be faulted for using a measure of the market risk premium based on one market index while using an estimate of β_L based on common-stock betas measured in relation to another stock-market index. Because the former index is a less risky one than the latter, the effect of this discrepancy is to reduce the allowed premium.

The CAPM itself has been the subject of a considerable amount of criticism of late. While some tests have questioned the validity of the simple version of the CAPM employed in the Fairley formula and in the present-value analysis presented here, the validity of these tests has also been questioned (see Roll 1977). If the simple version of the CAPM does indeed characterize security-market equilibrium, one would need a measure of beta based on the true market portfolio, a value-weighted portfolio of *all* risky assets, as well as the risk premium on this portfolio, in order to calculate a correct discount rate. Since it is virtually impossible to observe the complete market portfolio, estimated discount rates based on proxies for the market portfolio should be viewed with caution even when the proxy market portfolio is used consistently.

Notes

1. Expenses include both loss-adjustment expenses and underwriting expenses not paid at policy inception. This view of policy reserves differs from the usual statutory insurance accounting view of posting full nominal or undiscounted reserves for losses and expenses.

2. This equality holds at the time the policy is written. After the fact, losses and loss expenses may be higher or lower than anticipated. Thus equity holders may end up losers or winners. Nevertheless, as long as they cannot expect to win or lose consistently, they are playing a fair game.

3. Myers showed later, in the 1985 Massachusetts automobile rate hearings, that the present value of the tax on investment income does not depend on the risk of the securities held by the insurance company. It depends only on r_f, the risk-free interest rate, and on τ, the effective tax rate. Derrig (1985) reviews Myers's proof.

4. It is consistent with the analysis presented in Modigliani and Miller (1963).

5. For a recent analysis that leads to an "in-between" result, see DeAngelo and Masulis (1980).

6. The sample is necessarily small because only a few insurers have traded equity. Equity betas are required to estimate β_L by the method used in Massachusetts. Chapter 2 presents estimates of β_L for some of the traded companies.

References

DeAngelo, H., and R. W. Masulis. 1980. Optimal capital structure under corporate and personal taxation. *Journal of Financial Economics* 8(March):3–29.

Derrig, R. A. 1985. The effect of federal taxes on investment income in property-liability ratemaking. Working paper, Massachusetts Rating Bureau, Boston, MA.

Fairley, W. 1979. Investment income and profit margins in property-liability insurance: theory and empirical results. *Bell Journal of Economics* 10(Spring): 192–210.

Miller, M. H. 1977. Debt and taxes. *Journal of Finance* 32(May):261–275.

Modigliani, F., and M. H. Miller. 1963. Corporate income taxes and the cost of capital: a correction. *American Economic Review* 53(June):433–443.

Myers, S. C., and R. A. Cohn. 1981. Insurance rate of return regulation and the capital asset pricing model. Paper prepared for the Massachusetts automobile rate hearings, Boston, MA (August).

Roll, R. 1977. A critique of the asset pricing theory's tests; Part I: On past and potential testability of the theory. *Journal of Financial Economics* 4(March): 129–176.

Appendix: Development of the Model

This appendix provides formulas for the discounted cash flow model and illustrates the formulas using numerical examples. The resulting profit rates are compared with those implied by the Fairley model, described in chapter 1.[1]

Assumptions

Several important assumptions are incorporated in this model:

1. All cash flows occur at the beginnings of periods.
2. The insurance company commits surplus (equity capital) to provide financial backing for each policy. Surplus is committed according to a fixed ratio, S, the premiums-to-surplus ratio. Surplus is released as losses are paid. For example, if $S = 1.25$ and $P = \$100$, the initial surplus commitment is \$80—that is, $(1/S) \times \$100$. If half of the losses are paid one year after policy inception, the surplus commitment during the second year likewise declines by half, to \$40. The premiums-to-surplus ratio is assumed to be given exogenously—e.g., by the regulator.
3. Underwriting profits are accrued as losses are paid. Thus, if 20 percent of losses are paid at the beginning of any given period, 20 percent of underwriting profits are assumed to flow to the company and to be taxed at that time.
4. Premium inflows are nonstochastic and hence are discounted at the risk-free rate. Losses are discounted at a risk-adjusted discount rate, r_L. The variables appearing in the models are defined in table 3A-1.

The Discounted Cash Flow Model

In the discounted cash flow model, the present value of premiums should equal the present value of (1) loss and expense payments, (2) taxes on the investment balance, and (3) taxes on underwriting profits:

$$PV_{r_f}(P) = PV_{r_L}(L) + PV_{r_f}(IBT) + PV_{r_f,r_L}(UWPT) \qquad (3.4)$$

There are two discount rates for $UWPT$ because premiums are assumed certain and losses uncertain. The tax due to the premium is discounted at r_f, while the tax due to losses is discounted at r_L.

Formulas for the present values of premiums and losses are given below:

Table 3A-1. Definitions of Variables

r_f =	risk-free rate of interest
r_m =	required rate of return on the market portfolio
P =	total premiums
L =	total expected losses and expenses
τ =	corporate income-tax rate
S =	premiums-to-surplus ratio
β_L =	beta (systematic risk-coefficient) of losses and expenses
$PV_r(X)$ =	present value of the flow X discounted at the rate r
r_L =	discount rate for losses and expenses = $r_f + \beta_L(r_m - r_f)$
IB =	balance available for investment
IBT =	tax on investment income
UWP =	underwriting profit = $P - L$
$UWPT$ =	tax on underwriting profit = τUWP
π =	undiscounted underwriting profit rate = $(P - L)/P$
ϱ_i =	fraction of premiums received by the company at time i, $0 \leq \varrho_i \leq 1$, $\Sigma_i \varrho_i = 1$
l_i =	fraction of losses paid by the company at time i, $0 \leq l_i \leq 1$, $\Sigma_i l_i = 1$
i =	$0, 1, \ldots, N$, where 0 represents policy inception and N is the date of the last cash flow under the policy

$$\varkappa_1 = \sum_{i=0}^{N} \frac{\varrho_i}{(1 + r_f)^i}$$

$$\varkappa_2 = \sum_{i=0}^{N} \frac{l_i}{(1 + r_L)^i}$$

$$\varkappa_3 = \sum_{i=0}^{N-1} \frac{1}{(1 + r_f)^{i+1}} \left[\sum_{j=0}^{i} \varrho_i - \sum_{j=0}^{i} l_j + \left(\frac{1}{S}\right)\left(1 - \sum_{j=1}^{i} l_j\right) \right]$$

$$\varkappa_4 = \sum_{i=0}^{N} \frac{l_i}{(1 + r_f)^i}$$

$$PV_{r_f}(P) = \sum_{i=0}^{N} \frac{P\varrho_i}{(1 + r_f)^i} = P\varkappa_1 \quad (3.5)$$

$$PV_{r_L}(L) = \sum_{i=0}^{N} \frac{Ll_i}{(1 + r_L)^i} = L\varkappa_2 \tag{3.6}$$

It is usually assumed that no loss payments occur at time 0 and no premium payments occur at time N, that is, $l_0 = \varrho_N = 0$.

The investment balance (IB) is the amount of money, drawn from both premium and surplus, backing up the policy at any given time. It is set equal to the premiums that have been received, less the proportion of premiums matching the proportion of loss payments that have been made, plus the invested surplus committed to the policy. Committed surplus equals the original surplus times the proportion of losses yet unpaid. Thus,

$$IB_i = P\sum_{j=0}^{i} \varrho_j - P\sum_{j=0}^{i} l_j + P(1/S)\left(1 - \sum_{j=0}^{i} l_j\right) \tag{3.7}$$

The investment balance is assumed to earn interest during the period beginning at time i, and taxes are paid on this interest at the end of this period (i.e., at time $i + 1$). Thus,

$$IBT_{i+1} = IB_i r_f \tau,\ i = 0, 1 \ldots N - 1 \tag{3.8}$$

The investment balance tax is the tax on the investment earnings on IB_i. Thus,

$$\begin{aligned} PV_{r_f}(IBT) &= \sum_{i=0}^{N-1} \frac{IB_i r_f \tau}{(1 + r_f)^{i+1}} \\ &= Pr_f\tau \sum_{i=0}^{N-1} \frac{1}{(1 + r_f)^{i+1}}\left[\sum_{j=0}^{i} \varrho_j - \sum_{j=0}^{i} l_j + \left(1/S\right)\left(1 - \sum_{j=0}^{i} l_j\right)\right] \\ &= Pr_f\tau\varkappa_3 \end{aligned} \tag{3.9}$$

The underwriting profit, $UWP = P - L$, is assumed to emerge as losses are paid. Thus, the profit flow at time i, UWP_i, is $UWP \times l_i = (P - L)l_i$ and the present value of the underwriting profit is:

$$\begin{aligned} PV_{r_f,r_L}(UWP) &= PV_{r_f}(\text{premium component}) - PV_{r_L}\ (\text{loss component}) \\ &= P\sum_{i=0}^{N} \frac{l_i}{(1 + r_f)^i} - L\sum_{i=0}^{N} \frac{l_i}{(1 + r_L)^i} \\ &= P\varkappa_4 - L\varkappa_2 \end{aligned} \tag{3.10}$$

The present value of the loss component is identical to $PV_{r_f}(L)$, but the premium component differs from $PV_{r_f}(\mathrm{P})$ because premiums accrue for tax purposes when losses are paid rather than when premium payments are received.[2] The underwriting-profit tax at time i, $UWPT_i = \tau UWP_i$. The present value of the tax is then given by

$$PV_{r_f,r_L}(UWPT) = PV_{r_f,r_L}(UWP) \times \tau$$
$$= \tau P \varkappa_4 - \tau L \varkappa_2 \quad (3.11)$$

In the actual implementation of the model in Massachusetts, two tax rates are used, one applicable to investment income (τ_r) which is used to calculate the investment balance tax, and a second rate (τ_μ) which is used to calculate the underwriting profits tax.

The next step is to equate the present value of cash inflows with the present value of cash outflows:

$$PV_{r_f}(P) = PV_{r_L}(L) + PV_{r_f}(IBT) + PV_{r_f,r_L}(UWPT)$$

Substituting from equations (3.5), (3.6), (3.9), and (3.11), one obtains

$$P\varkappa_1 = L\varkappa_2 + Pr_f\tau\varkappa_3 + P\tau\varkappa_4 - L\tau\varkappa_2$$

This expression is then solved for P/L:

$$\frac{P}{L} = \frac{\varkappa_2(1 - \tau)}{\varkappa_1 - r_f\tau\varkappa_3 - \tau\varkappa_4} \quad (3.12)$$

This ratio is multiplied by expected losses and expenses to yield the fair premium.

The model treats underwriting profits and losses symmetrically for tax purposes: underwriting profits are taxable, and losses generate tax shields. Tax shields from underwriting losses are used to offset taxes on investment income or taxes on the insurance company's other policies or activities.

Fairley's Model

Fairley develops an alternative formula for the underwriting profit margin (see chapter 1). This profit rate represents the present value (at policy inception) of the underwriting profit margin and is called the *discounted profit margin* in this appendix. The formula for the discounted profit margin (p) is:

$$p = -kr_f - k\beta_L(r_m - r_f) + \frac{\tau r_f}{(1 - \tau)S} \quad (3.13)$$

The first term on the right of equation (3.13) is the payment to the policyholders (at the risk-free rate) for the use of their funds during the period between the receipt of premiums and the payment of losses. The second term compensates the company for the systematic risk of underwriting, while the third term is an adjustment for taxes.

Fairley defined k as "the average amount of investable funds created by the cash flow per dollar of annual premium" (chapter 1, p. 6). More precisely,

$$kr_f = \sum_{i=0}^{N} \frac{\varrho_i}{(1 + r_f)^i} - \sum_{i=0}^{N} \frac{l_i}{(1 + r_f)^i} \tag{3.14}$$

The right-hand side of equation (3.14) can be roughly interpreted as the difference between the present value of the policyholder's payments to the company and the payments he or she expects to receive from the company. However, note that the present value of losses is calculated at the risk-free rate r_f, not the risk-adjusted rate appropriate for them. Also, cash inflows and outflows are expressed per dollar of expected losses. That is, underwriting profits are implicitly excluded from policyholders' payments to the company.

The discounted profit margin is related to the undiscounted profit margin $\pi = (P - L)/P$ as follows:

$$p = \pi \sum_{i=0}^{N} \frac{l_i}{(1 + r_f)^i} \tag{3.15}$$

In an actual ratemaking application, π would be used rather than p. Thus, for comparison with the Myers-Cohn model we use $P/L = 1/(1 - \pi)$, where π is computed from equation (3.15) and p and k are computed using equations (3.13) and (3.14).

Numerical Examples

A. Two-Period Example. The parameter values and cash flow rates for the two-period example are given in table 3A-2. Using these values and equation (3.12), one obtains

$$\frac{P}{L} = \frac{(1 - 0.4)(1/1.082)}{1.0 - (0.08/1.10) - (0.4/1.10)}$$

$$= \frac{0.9242 - 0.3697}{1.0 - 0.0727 - 0.3636}$$

$$= 0.9837$$

Using Fairley's formulas, (3.13), (3.14), and (3.15):

Table 3A-2. Parameter Values and Cash Flow Rates for the Two-Period Example

Parameter Values

$r_f = 0.10$	$r_L = 0.082$	$\tau = 0.40$
$r_m - r_f = 0.09$	$\beta_L = -0.20$	$S = 1.0$

Cash Flow Rates

	Period	
Rate[a]	*0*	*1*
ϱ_i	1	0
l_i	0	1
IB_i/P	2	0
IBT_i/P	0	0.08
$UWP_i/(P - L)$	0	1
$UWPT_i/(P - L)$	0	0.4

[a] i = period.

$$k = \frac{1}{0.1}\left(1 - \frac{1}{1.1}\right) = 0.9091$$

$$p = -0.9091(0.10) - 0.9091(-0.20)(0.09) + \frac{0.4(0.10)}{(1 - 0.4)1.0}$$

$$= -0.09091 + 0.0164 + 0.0667 = -0.0079$$

$$\pi = \frac{-0.0079}{(1/1.1)} = -0.0087$$

$$\frac{P}{L} = \frac{1}{1 - (-0.0087)} = 0.9914$$

B. Five-Quarter Example. The parameter values and cash flow rates for a policy in which the cash flows cover five periods are shown in table 3A-3. The data in the table can be used to obtain the fair premium. As indicated in the table, these calculations yield

$$\frac{P}{L} = \frac{0.9653(1 - 0.2)}{0.9807 - 0.0117 - 0.1912} = 0.9928$$

for the Myers-Cohn model. Similar calculations underlie the results presented in tables 3-5 and 3-6 of the text.

Table 3A-4 has been prepared to provide a better understanding of cash

Table 3A-3. Parameter Values and Cash Flow Rates and Resulting *P/L* Ratios for the Five-Quarter Example

Parameter Values

$r_f = 0.0199$ per quarter $\quad r_L = 0.0155$ per quarter $\quad \tau = 0.20$

$r_m - r_f = 0.0213$ per quarter $\quad \beta_L = -0.21 \quad S = 1.30$

Cash Flow Rates

Rate[a]	Quarter 0	1	2	3	4
ϱ_i	0.4	0.3	0.2	0.1	0
l_i	0	0.2	0.4	0.3	0.1
IB_i/P	1.169	1.115	0.608	0.177	0
IBT_i/P	0	0.0047	0.0044	0.0024	0.0007
$UWP_i/(P - L)$	0	0.2	0.4	0.3	0.1
$UWPT_i/(P - L)$	0	0.04	0.08	0.06	0.02

[a] i = quarter.

Myers-Cohn Model:

$$\frac{P}{L} = \frac{0.9653(1 - 0.2)}{0.9807 - 0.0117 - 0.1912} = 0.9928$$

Fairley's Method:*

$k = 0.3029$

$$p = -0.3029(0.082) - (0.3029)(-0.21)(0.088) + \frac{0.4(0.082)}{(1 - 0.4)(1.3)} = 0.02281$$

$$\pi = \frac{0.0228}{0.95584} = 0.02385$$

$$\frac{P}{L} = \frac{1}{1 - (0.02385)} = 1.0244$$

* Fairley's method uses *annual* rates of interest and, therefore, we take: $r_f = (1.0199)^4 - 1 = 0.082$ and $r_m - r_f = (1.0213)^4 - 1 = 0.088$.

flow patterns under the discounted cash flow model. The table assumes that flows occur according to table 3A-3 and that losses (L) = \$100. Thus, the premium is \$99.28. The table breaks down the resulting flows into inflows, outflows, the investment balance, and shareholder flows.

Premiums are assumed paid in the time-pattern given in table 3A-3

		Period				
		0	*1*	*2*	*3*	*4*
	Inflows					
(1)	Premium	$ 39.71	$ 29.78	$19.86	$ 9.93	$ 0.00
(2)	Surplus	76.37	0.00	0.00	0.00	0.00
(3)	Investment income	0.00	2.31	2.20	1.20	0.35
(4)	Underwriting tax credit	0.00	0.03	0.06	0.04	0.01
(5)	Total [(1) + (2) + (3) + (4)]	116.08	32.12	22.12	11.17	0.36
	Outflows					
(6)	Losses	$ 0.00	$ 20.00	$40.00	$30.00	$10.00
(7)	Surplus	0.00	15.27	30.55	22.91	7.64
(8)	Investment income tax	0.00	0.46	0.44	0.24	0.07
(9)	Income on surplus [(10) + (11)]	0.00	1.77	1.47	0.81	0.22
(10)	{Investment income}	{0.00}	{1.52}	{1.22}	{0.61}	{0.15}
(11)	{Operating income}	{0.00}	{0.25}	{0.25}	{0.20}	{0.07}
(12)	Total [(6) + (7) + (8) + (9)]	0.00	37.50	72.46	53.96	17.93
	Investment Balance					
(13)	Surplus	$ 76.37	$ 61.10	$30.55	$ 7.64	$ 0.00
(14)	Operations	39.71	49.60	29.81	9.93	0.00
(15)	Total [(15) + (5) − (12)]	116.08	110.70	60.36	17.57	0.00
	Shareholder Flows					
(16)	Surplus	$−76.37	$ 15.27	$30.55	$22.91	$ 7.64
(17)	Investment income (10)	0.00	1.52	1.22	0.61	0.15
(18)	Operating income (11)	0.00	0.25	0.25	0.20	0.07
(19)	Total [(16) + (17) + (18)]	−76.37	17.04	32.02	23.72	7.86

[a] Table entries are based on the following assumptions: premium (P) = $99.28, surplus ($P/S$) = $76.37 = $99.28 × $(1.3)^{-1}$, and losses (L) = $100. Other assumptions are presented in table 3A-3.

(ϱ_i). Surplus is contributed at time zero at the premiums-to-surplus ratio (S) assumed in table 3A-3. No further surplus inflows take place, and the initial surplus contribution is drawn down (returned to the company) as losses are paid (i.e., in proportion to the l_i). Investment income at time i is equal to the investment balance (the sum of unreturned surplus and unexpended premiums) at time $i - 1$, multiplied by the assumed risk-free rate, 0.0199 per quarter. Finally, the underwriting tax credit is given by

$$(P - L) \times \tau \times l_i \tag{3.16}$$

The underwriting tax credit is an inflow because $(P - L)$ is negative. The implicit assumption is that the company can fully recapture the tax credit, either as an offset to taxes on investment income or to taxes on income from the company's other policies or activities.

Outflows include loss payments and funds released from surplus. The latter are assumed to flow out of the account and back to the company. Surplus released at time i is l_i multiplied by initial surplus. The investment income tax, another outflow, is investment income [row (3)] multiplied by the tax rate (τ).

Income on surplus [row (9)] is the amount the company can withdraw from the account, while maintaining the target investment balance in the account. Hence, it is obtained as follows:

$$\begin{aligned} \text{income on surplus}_i = {} & \text{total inflows}_i - Ll_i - (P/S)l_i \\ & - r_f IB_{i-1} - (IB_i - IB_{i-1}) \end{aligned} \tag{3.17}$$

Income on surplus is broken down between investment income [row (10)] and operating income [row (11)]. Investment income in period i is the prior period's surplus [row (13)] multiplied by the risk-free rate. Operating income is the difference between income on surplus [row (9)] and investment income on surplus [row (10)].

Rows (13) through (15) give the investment balance. Row (13) is governed by the third term on the right-hand side of equation (3.7), while row (14) is calculated using the first two terms on the right-hand side of that equation.

The final section of table 3A-4 summarizes the flows to shareholders. Row (16) gives the surplus flows, which are equal to row (2) minus row (7). Rows (17) and (18) contain the two components of income on surplus, investment income and operating income.

Table 3A-5 categorizes the flows of the five-period example into operating and investment flows. Most of the entries in the table are identical to those in table 3A-4. The operating flows consist of premiums,

Table 3A-5. Cash flows off Five-Quarter Example Categorized as Operating and Investment Flows[a]

		Period				
		0	1	2	3	4
	Operating Flows					
(1)	Premiums	$ 39.71	$ 29.78	$ 19.86	$ 9.93	$ 0.00
(2)	Losses	0.00	20.00	40.00	30.00	10.00
(3)	Underwriting tax	0.00	−0.03	−0.06	−0.04	−0.01
(4)	Total [(1) − (2) − (3)]	39.71	9.81	−20.08	−20.03	−9.99
	Investment Flows					
(5)	Required total investment balance	$ 116.08	$ 110.70	$ 60.36	$ 17.57	$ 0.00
(6)	Required surplus included in (5)	76.37	61.10	30.55	7.64	0.00
(7)	Withdrawal from required total investment balance; negative value indicates required contribution [(7) = change in (5)]	−116.08	5.38	50.34	42.79	17.57
(8)	After-tax investment income on total investment balance	0.00	1.85	1.76	0.96	0.28
(9)	Total cash flow from investment balance [(7) + (8)]	−116.08	7.23	52.10	43.75	17.85
	Cash Flows To Investors					
(10)	From operations (4)	$ 39.71	$ 9.81	$ −20.08	$ −20.03	$ −9.99
(11)	From investment (9)	−116.08	7.23	52.10	43.75	17.85
(12)	Total [(10) + (11)]	−76.37	17.04	32.02	23.72	7.86
	Profit To Investors					
(13)	Cash flow	$ −76.37	$ 17.04	$ 32.02	$ 23.72	$ 7.86
(14)	Increase in required surplus	76.37	−15.27	−30.55	−22.91	−7.64
(15)	Realized profit [(13) + (14)]	0.00	1.77	1.47	0.81	0.22

[a] Table entries are based on the following assumptions: premium (P) = \$99.28, surplus (P/S) = \$76.37 = \$99.28 × $(1.3)^{-1}$, and losses (L) = \$100. Other assumptions are presented in table 3A-3.

losses, and the underwriting tax credit. The investment flows are summarized in rows (7) and (8). Row (7) presents the flows into and out of the required investment balance, while row (8) is the after-tax investment income on the investment balance. The total cash flow from the investment balance is shown in row (9). Rows (5) and (6) are presented to show the amount and composition of the investment balance.

Cash flows to investors [rows (10) and (11)] include the operating flows and the investment flows, while investors' profit [row (15)] is the sum of the cash flows and the increase in required surplus. Negative cash flows are amounts flowing from the investors into the insurance account, while positive cash flows come from the account to investors. Since part of each cash flow in row (13) represents surplus backing supplied by the investors, this amount must be deducted in order to obtain the profit.

Notes to Appendix 3A

Editor's note: The discounted cash flow model described in this chapter, with some modifications, has been implemented for automobile and workers' compensation rate making in Massachusetts. It has come to be known as the *Myers-Cohn* or *surplus flow model*.

1. This appendix is based on tables, examples, and other materials prepared for several years' Massachusetts automobile rate hearings by the authors and by Richard Derrig of the Massachusetts Rating Bureau. The authors wish to thank Dr. Derrig and the Bureau for permission to use these materials. The authors also wish to thank the editor, J. David Cummins, for helping assemble these materials in a readable unit. Professor Cummins put together an excellent first draft of this appendix.

2. This is an economic view of tax liability timing. Current Internal Revenue Service regulations require that premiums be recognized as earned and losses and expenses as incurred. This requirement has been modeled in Massachusetts as a uniform flow in quarters 1 to 4.

4 INSURANCE IN AN EQUILIBRIUM ASSET-PRICING MODEL

Andrew L. Turner

This chapter presents a model of the demand for insurance company shares and insurance policies. Individuals in the model respond to uncertainty about real assets by purchasing insurance policies and insurance company shares. Insurance firms arise naturally in the model as risk-sharing devices. This chapter analyzes the nature of individual demand functions to establish equilibrium prices for insurance policies and insurance shares. Although the chapter focuses on insurance activity, equilibrium prices for securities and real assets also are derived.

Several past works on insurance have indicated that insurance decisions are simple extensions of other portfolio decisions (e.g., Hakansson 1969; Dreze and Modigliani 1972; Fischer 1973; and Richard 1975). This chapter reexamines this question and, in particular, investigates the nature of portfolio separation properties in an insurance market. In contrast to the results of Richard (1975), portfolio decisions do not exhibit multiple fund separation. Essentially, due to the nature of the insurable and insured risks, each individual desires a unique portfolio of securities, real assets, insurance policies, and insurance shares.

Table 4-1. Symbols Appearing in the Model

Symbol	*Definition*
Subscripts:	
$f = 1, \ldots, F$	Insurance companies
$h = 1, \ldots, H$	Individuals or households
$i = 1, \ldots, I$	Firms engaged in production (productive firms)
$k = 1, \ldots, K$	Real assets
Variables:[a]	
V_i	Initial (beginning of period) price of one share in productive firm i
$\tilde{R}_i$	Cash flow per share of stock i
v_{hi}	Number of shares in productive firm i owned by household h
v_{fi}	Number of shares in productive firm i owned by insurance company f
A_k	Initial (beginning of period) price of one real asset of type k
$\tilde{R}_k$	Cash flow attributable to market risk on one real asset of type k
$\tilde{L}_k$	Social losses, i.e., negative cash flow, of real assets of type k due to social hazards
$\tilde{X}_{hk}$	Individual losses, i.e., negative cash flow of real assets of type k due to individual hazards of household h
a_{hk}	Number of real assets of type k owned by household h
S_f	Initial (beginning of period) price of one share in insurance firm f
$\tilde{Y}_f$	Cash flow per share of insurance firm f
s_{hf}	Number of shares in insurance firm f owned by household h
P_{fk}	Premium per unit of insurance in asset type k charged by insurance firm f
n_{hfk}	Number of units of insurance in asset type k purchased by household h from insurance firm f
c_{fk}	Coverage ratio (percentage of any loss borne by the insurer) of insurance firm f for asset type k

Table 4-1. *(continued)*

Symbol	*Definition*
W_h	Initial (beginning of period) wealth of household h
$\tilde{W}_h$	Terminal (end of period) wealth of household h
C_h	Current consumption of household h
μ_h	Expected value of terminal wealth of individual h
ν_h	Variance of terminal wealth of individual h

[a] Tildes denote randomness.

Model Scenario

This section establishes the scenario for the asset-pricing model used in this chapter. The symbols appearing in the model are defined in table 4-1.

Consider an economy in which individuals or households, indexed by $h = 1, \ldots, H$, own marketable assets of two types: financial assets issued by corporations engaged in production (hereinafter denoted stocks) and real, tangible assets. Individual h may purchase the number of shares v_{hi} in productive firm $i(i = 1, \ldots, I)$ at the price V_i. Ownership of stock i entitles the individual to the uncertain cash flows $\tilde{R}_i$. The supplies of all stocks are taken as given with the production decisions of each firm fixed throughout the analysis.

Each individual may also purchase a_{hk} real assets having initial value A_k for the kth real asset type ($k = 1, 2, \ldots, K$). This may be interpreted in the following way: individual h purchases a_{hk} units of asset k (e.g., housing) where the price of one unit of asset k is A_k. The individual's total investment in asset k is $a_{hk}A_k$. Each real asset is assumed to be fully marketable and divisible.

Unlike stocks, real assets are subject to two sources of uncertainty surrounding their future market value. Like stocks, real assets may experience changes in market value related to changes in technology and the general economy. This type of market value change is denoted *market risk*. To emphasize the essential similarity between this risk and the stock market risks, the cash flow attributable to the market risk of the real asset k is denoted $\tilde{R}_k$.

In addition to the market risk $\tilde{R}_k$, real assets are subject to nonmarket risks. These risks are causally unrelated to production and include natural hazard losses to property (e.g., fire, theft, accident, etc.). These losses occur in two forms, social losses $\tilde{L}_k$ and individual losses $\tilde{X}_{hk}$. The variable $\tilde{L}_k$ represents the social nonmarket risk of asset k, the uncertainty common to all owners of type k assets, whereas $\tilde{X}_{hk}$ represents the individual risk of asset k attributable to ownership by individual h. Individual h's total return on real asset k is $a_{hk}(\tilde{R}_k - \tilde{L}_k - \tilde{X}_{hk})$. Holding the supply of real assets fixed, these definitions of $\tilde{L}_k$ and $\tilde{X}_{hk}$ correspond to the commonly employed definitions of social and individual risk (Arrow and Lind 1970; Brainard and Dolbear 1971; Kihlstrom and Pauly 1971; and Malinvaud 1971).

Faced with these sources of uncertainty to their wealth, some individuals attempt to reduce or diversify these risks. One possible response is to avoid nonmarket losses by leasing real assets. However, leasing also shifts market returns, as well as nonmarket returns, to the lessor. As an alternative to leasing, or complete avoidance of real assets, some individuals form insurance companies to exploit the higher risk aversion or personal characteristics of individuals desiring to purchase insurance policies.

Once formed, insurance firm $f (f = 1, 2, \ldots, F)$ sells s_{hf} shares with initial value S_f to individual h. Simultaneously, the firm sells insurance policies to individuals desiring insurance against nonmarket losses.[1] The random cash flow resulting from ownership of an insurance share is $\tilde{Y}_f$. As a result of insurance company budget constraints, the cash flows $\tilde{Y}_f$ are linear combinations of the stock returns $\tilde{R}_i$ and the nonmarket losses of the real assets $\tilde{L}_k$ and $\tilde{X}_{hk}$.

Each individual may purchase insurance in type k real assets from any insurers. Individuals are not restricted to purchasing insurance from only one firm. The number of units of insurance purchased by individual h from firm f is n_{hfk}. The premium charged by firm f for assets of type k is P_{fk}. Funds held by insurer f are invested in v_{fi} shares of productive firm $i (i = 1, 2, \ldots, I)$ pending the payment of claims. Should a loss of size $\tilde{L}_k + \tilde{X}_{hk}$ occur, the insurance company will pay $c_{fk}(\tilde{L}_k + \tilde{X}_{hk})$ to individual h per unit of insurance. The variable c_{fk} represents the coverage ratio of the firm for line k insurance. It may be interpreted as a coinsurance rate with the insurer covering $100c_{fk}$ percent of any loss and the insured self-insuring any residual. Total claim payments received by household h on asset k would be $\Sigma_f n_{hfk} c_{fk}(\tilde{L}_k + \tilde{S}_{hk})$.

Full insurance on any asset implies that

$$\sum_f n_{hfk} c_{fk} = a_{hk} \tag{4.1}$$

Insureds may avoid full insurance either by purchasing policies where $c_{fk} < 1$ or by purchasing insurance on an amount less than the asset's value. It is assumed that

$$\sum_f n_{hfk} c_{fk} \leqslant a_{hk} \tag{4.2}$$

so that households cannot overinsure. This assumption allows the model to avoid some questions of moral hazard.[2]

Households begin the period with initial wealth W_h. They may freely allocate this wealth among stocks (securities of productive firms), real assets, insurance shares, insurance policies, and current consumption, C_h. At the end of the period, the households receive returns on their asset holdings, resulting in terminal wealth $\tilde{W}_h$. Each household selects the consumption (C_h) and savings ($\{v_{hi}\}$, $\{s_{hf}\}$, $\{a_{hk}\}$, $\{n_{hfk}\}$) plan that maximizes utility. All purchase and sale orders are tentative, with recontracting taking place until all agents in the various markets have zero excess demands. Under this tatonnement process, insurance demands and supplies are endogenous to the model.

In the model, insurance firms act as brokerage operations. This activity is not costless and households wishing to purchase insurance must ultimately bear these brokerage costs. Individual insurance shareholders expect returns commensurate with the costs and risks of forming the insurance firms. Insurance shareholders treat the insurance shares as they would any other residual claim on the cash flows of a firm. While the risk and return characteristics of insurance firms may differ from those of productive firms, ownership of insurance shares clearly is identical in principle to ownership of any other security.

Households in the model purchase insurance policies to remove certain types of real-asset risks. These policies are also securities with their own risk and return characteristics. They do not differ substantively from insurance shares or stocks. When forming a consumption-savings plan, households view insurance shares and policies, stocks, and real assets as claims on cash flows that are imperfectly substitutable only because of their risk and return properties. Thus, by treating insurance assets as securities without according them special a priori properties, the model's conclusions result from the interaction of the insurance process with individual consumption-savings plans.

Asset Demands

Problem Statement

Each individual agent (household) selects a consumption-savings plan to maximize its expected utility subject to a budget constraint. These plans are selected in an environment essentially free of frictions in the trading process. The assumptions employed in the model are formalized thus:

- A.1 The asset markets are perfectly competitive with all agents accepting the ruling market prices as given.
- A.2 There are no transactions costs or taxes involving the possession or transfer of assets.
- A.3 There are no restrictions on the use of short sales.
- A.4 All agents have homogeneous expectations concerning all relevant probability distributions.
- A.5 All households are risk averse, one-period utility maximizers whose preferences can be described in terms of means and variances.[3]

Each individual faces a budget constraint on his initial wealth W_h such that

$$W_h = \sum_i v_{hi} V_i + \sum_k a_{hk} A_k + \sum_f s_{hf} S_f + \sum_{fk} n_{hfk} P_{fk} + C_h \qquad (4.3)$$

where the symbols are defined in table 4-1. The random cash flows accruing to individual h are equal to

$$\tilde{W}_h = \sum_i v_{hi} \tilde{R}_i + \sum_k a_{hk} (\tilde{R}_k - \tilde{L}_k - \tilde{X}_{hk}) + \sum_f s_{hf} \tilde{Y}_f + \sum_{fk} n_{hfk} c_{fk} (\tilde{L}_k + \tilde{X}_{hk}) \qquad (4.4)$$

Denoting expected values by bars, the expected terminal wealth for individual h, (μ_h) is given by

$$\mu_h = \sum_i v_{hi} \bar{R}_i + \sum_f s_{hf} \bar{Y}_f + \sum_k a_{hk} (\bar{R}_k - \bar{L}_k - \bar{X}_{hk}) + \sum_{fk} n_{hfk} c_{fk} (\bar{L}_k + \bar{X}_{hk}) \qquad (4.5)$$

The variance of terminal wealth, ν_h, dropping the tildes for simplicity, is given by

$$\nu_h = \sum_{ij} v_{hi} v_{hj} \operatorname{cov}(R_i, R_j) + 2 \sum_{if} v_{hi} s_{hf} \operatorname{cov}(R_i, Y_f)$$

$$+ 2\sum_{ik} v_{hi}a_{hk}\,\mathrm{cov}(R_i,R_k - L_k - X_{hk})$$

$$+ 2\sum_{ifk} v_{hi}n_{hfk}c_{fk}\,\mathrm{cov}(R_i,L_k + X_{hk}) + \sum_{fg} s_{hf}s_{hg}\,\mathrm{cov}(Y_f,Y_g)$$

$$+ 2\sum_{fk} s_{hf}a_{hk}\,\mathrm{cov}(Y_f,R_k - L_k - X_{hk})$$

$$+ 2\sum_{gfk} s_{hg}n_{hfk}c_{fk}\,\mathrm{cov}(Y_g,L_k + X_{hk})$$

$$+ \sum_{kl} a_{hk}a_{hl}\,\mathrm{cov}(R_k - L_k - X_{hk},R_l - L_l - X_{hl})$$

$$+ 2\sum_{lfk} a_{hl}n_{hfk}c_{fk}\,\mathrm{cov}(R_l - L_l - X_{hl},L_k - X_{hk})$$

$$+ \sum_{fkgl} n_{hfk}c_{fk}n_{hgl}c_{gl}\,\mathrm{cov}(L_k + X_{hk},L_l + X_{hl}) \tag{4.6}$$

Although the $\tilde{X}_{hk}$ are mutually independent for all h and k, it is more convenient to eliminate the $\tilde{X}_{hk}$ at a later point in the analysis. This helps to demonstrate that the independence assumption is not critical to the development or conclusions of the model.

Household h seeks to maximize a utility function U_h subject to the budget constraint (4.3). The utility function U_h depends on the mean and variance of terminal wealth as well as on consumption.[4] The maximization problem may be formalized as

$$\max_{\{v_{hi},s_{hf},a_{hk},n_{hfk},C_h\}} U_h(\mu_h,\nu_h,C_h)$$

$$- \psi_h\left(\sum_i v_{hi}V_i + \sum_f s_{hf}S_f + \sum_k a_{hk}A_k + \sum_{fk} n_{hfk}P_{fk} + C_h - W_h\right) \tag{4.7}$$

where ψ_h is a Lagrange multiplier.

First Order Conditions

To simplify the notation define U'_μ, U'_ν, and U'_C as the partial derivatives

$$U'_\mu = \partial U_h/\partial \mu_h \qquad U'_\nu = \partial U_h/\partial \nu_h \qquad U'_C = \partial U_h/\partial C_h$$

dropping the subscripts on the utility function for convenience. The first-order conditions for the optimization problem (4.7) are

$$0 = \bar{R}_i U'_\mu + 2U'_\nu \operatorname{cov}\left[R_i, \sum_j v_{hj}R_j + \sum_f s_{hf}Y_f + \sum_k a_{hk}(R_k - L_k - X_{hk}) + \sum_{fk} n_{hfk}c_{fk}(L_k + X_{hk})\right] - \psi_h V_i \tag{4.8}$$

$$0 = \bar{Y}_f U'_\mu + 2U'_\nu \operatorname{cov}\left[Y_f, \sum_i v_{hi}R_i + \sum_g s_{hg}Y_g + \sum_k a_{hk}(R_k - L_k - X_{hk}) + \sum_{gk} n_{hgk}c_{gk}(L_k + X_{hk})\right] - \psi_h S_f \tag{4.9}$$

$$0 = (\bar{R}_k - \bar{L}_k - \bar{X}_{hk})U'_\mu + 2U'_\nu \operatorname{cov}\left[R_k - L_k - X_{hk}, \sum_i v_{hi}R_i + \sum_f s_{hf}Y_f + \sum_l a_{hl}(R_l - L_l - X_{hl}) + \sum_{gl} n_{hgl}c_{gl}(L_l + X_{hl})\right] - \psi_h A_k \tag{4.10}$$

$$0 = (\bar{L}_k + \bar{X}_{hk})c_{fk}U'_\mu + 2U'_\nu c_{fk} \operatorname{cov}\left[L_k + X_{hk}, \sum_i v_{hi}R_i + \sum_g s_{hg}Y_g + \sum_l a_{hl}(R_l - L_l - X_{hl}) + \sum_{gl} n_{hgl}c_{gl}(L_l + X_{hl})\right] - \psi_h P_{fk} \tag{4.11}$$

$$0 = U'_C - \psi_h \tag{4.12}$$

The condition (4.12) permits a simple solution for ψ_h and at the same time provides an intuitive rationale for the pricing equations.

Define the new variables λ_h and θ_h as

$$\lambda_h \equiv U'_\nu/U'_\mu = \partial\mu_h/\partial\nu_h \tag{4.13}$$

$$\theta_h \equiv U'_C/U'_\nu = \delta\nu_h/\delta C_h \tag{4.14}$$

The marginal rate of substitution of risk for return is measured by λ_h, while θ_h is the marginal rate of substitution of consumption for risk. In the presence of a riskless asset, $\lambda_h = \lambda$ for all h. As long as a riskless asset exists with unrestricted borrowing, the marginal rates of substitution of risk for return must be equal across all households. In the absence of a riskless asset, as in the model presented here, the λ_h differs across households. The marginal rate of substitution of consumption for risk, θ_h, is unrestricted across households regardless of the presence or absence of a riskless asset.

In the system represented by equations (4.8) through (4.11), replace ψ_h with U'_C using equation (4.12) and divide by U'_v, employing the definitions (4.13) and (4.14). The first-order conditions can be written as

$$0 = \lambda_h^{-1}\bar{R}_i - \theta_h V_i + 2\,\mathrm{cov}\Bigg[R_i, \sum_j v_{hj}R_j + \sum_f s_{hf}Y_f + \sum_k a_{hk}(R_k - L_k - X_{hk}) + \sum_{fk} n_{hfk}c_{fk}(L_k + X_{hk})\Bigg] \tag{4.15}$$

$$0 = \lambda_h^{-1}\bar{Y}_f - \theta_h S_f + 2\,\mathrm{cov}\Bigg[Y_f, \sum_i v_{hi}R_i + \sum_g s_{hg}Y_g + \sum_k a_{hk}(R_k - L_k - X_{hk}) + \sum_{gk} n_{hgk}c_{gk}(L_k + X_{hk})\Bigg] \tag{4.16}$$

$$0 = \lambda_h^{-1}(\bar{R}_k - \bar{L}_k - \bar{X}_{hk}) - \theta_h A_k + 2\,\mathrm{cov}\Bigg[R_k - L_k - X_{hk}, \sum_i v_{hi}R_i + \sum_f s_{hf}Y_f + \sum_l a_{hl}(R_l - L_l - X_{hl}) + \sum_{gl} n_{hgl}c_{gl}(L_l + X_{hl})\Bigg] \tag{4.17}$$

$$0 = \lambda_h^{-1}(\bar{L}_k - \bar{X}_{hk}) - \theta_h (P_{fk}/c_{fk}) + 2\,\mathrm{cov}\Bigg[L_k - X_{hk}, \sum_i v_{hi}R_i + \sum_g s_{hg}Y_g + \sum_l a_{hl}(R_l - L_l - X_{hl}) + \sum_{gl} n_{hgl}c_{gl}(L_l + X_{hl})\Bigg] \tag{4.18}$$

The system represented by equations (4.15) through (4.18) has an interesting feature. The first two terms in each equation involve constants times single terms in h. Each covariance term has a similar property. Thus, it is possible to aggregate conditions (4.15) through (4.18) without assuming that either $\lambda_h = \lambda$ for all h or that $\theta_h = \theta$ for all h. Households are free to have completely different marginal rates of substitution.[5]

Aggregation of Individual Demands

Aggregating the system represented by equations (4.15) through (4.18) leads to the conditions.

$$0 = \left(\sum_h \lambda_h^{-1}\right)\bar{R}_i - \left(\sum_h \theta_h\right)V_i + 2\,\mathrm{cov}\left[R_i, \sum_{hj} v_{hj}R_j + \sum_{hf} s_{hf}Y_f + \sum_{hk} a_{hk}(R_k - L_k - X_{hk}) + \sum_{hfk} n_{hfk}c_{fk}(L_k + X_{hk})\right] \tag{4.19}$$

$$0 = \left(\sum_h \lambda_h^{-1}\right)\bar{Y}_f - \left(\sum_h \theta_h\right)S_f + 2\,\mathrm{cov}\left[Y_f, \sum_{hi} v_{hi}R_i + \sum_{hg} s_{hg}Y_g + \sum_{hk} a_{hk}(R_k - L_k - X_{hk}) + \sum_{hgk} n_{hgk}c_{gk}(L_k + X_{hk})\right] \tag{4.20}$$

$$0 = \left(\sum_h \lambda_h^{-1}\right)(\bar{R}_k - \bar{L}_k - \bar{X}_k) - \left(\sum_h \theta_h\right)A_k + 2\sum_h \mathrm{cov}\left[R_k - L_k - X_{hk}, \sum_i v_{hi}R_i + \sum_g s_{hg}Y_g + \sum_l a_{hl}(R_l - L_l - X_{hl}) + \sum_{gl} n_{hgl}c_{gl}(L_l + X_{hl})\right] \tag{4.21}$$

$$0 = \left(\sum_h \lambda_h^{-1}\right)(\bar{L}_k - \bar{X}_k) - \left(\sum_h \theta_h\right)\left(P_{fk}/c_{fk}\right) + 2\sum_h \mathrm{cov}\left[L_k + X_{hk}, \sum_i v_{hi}R_i + \sum_g s_{hg}Y_g + \sum_l a_{hl}(R_l - L_l - X_{hl}) + \sum_{gl} n_{hgl}c_{gl}(L_l + X_{hl})\right] \tag{4.22}$$

where $\bar{X}_k$ is defined as

$$\bar{X}_h = \frac{\sum_h \lambda_h^{-1}\bar{X}_{hk}}{\sum_h \lambda_h^{-1}} \tag{4.23}$$

In equation (4.19), aggregation was possible because $\bar{R}_i$ is independent of h. The summed covariance is the covariance of stock i with the total asset ownership of all households.

Since the insurance system is closed, someone must hold insurance shares if insurance policies are sold. Therefore, it should be possible to simplify equation (4.19) further. For an individual insurance firm f, the final value of the equity is given by

$$\sum_h s_{hf}\tilde{Y}_f = \sum_i v_{fi}\tilde{R}_i - \sum_{hk} n_{hfk}c_{fk}(\tilde{L}_k + \tilde{X}_{hk}) \tag{4.24}$$

The total equity value of the insurance sector is

$$\sum_{hf} s_{hf}\tilde{Y}f = \sum_{fi} v_{fi}\tilde{R}_i - \sum_{hfk} n_{hfk}c_{fk}(\tilde{\mathrm{L}}_{\mathrm{k}} + \tilde{\mathrm{X}}_{\mathrm{hk}}) \tag{4.25}$$

Define new insurance sector variables $\tilde{Y}_I$, $\tilde{L}_I$, and $\tilde{X}_I$ such that

$$\tilde{Y}_I = \sum_{hf} s_{hf}\tilde{Y}_f \tag{4.26}$$

$$\tilde{L}_I = \sum_{hfk} n_{hfk}c_{fk}\tilde{L}_k \tag{4.27}$$

$$\tilde{X}_I = \sum_{hfk} n_{hfk}c_{fk}\tilde{X}_{hk} \tag{4.28}$$

Using these definitions, total insurance-sector equity is

$$\tilde{Y}_I = \sum_{fi} v_{fi}\tilde{R}_i - (\tilde{L}_I + \tilde{X}_I) \tag{4.29}$$

Define the real asset aggregates $\tilde{R}_N$, $\tilde{L}_N$, and $\tilde{X}_N$ such that

$$\tilde{R}_N = \sum_{hk} a_{hk}\tilde{R}_k \tag{4.30}$$

$$\tilde{L}_N = \sum_{hk} a_{hk}\tilde{L}_k \tag{4.31}$$

$$\tilde{X}_N = \sum_{hk} a_{hk}\tilde{X}_{hx} \tag{4.32}$$

$\tilde{L}_N$ represents total social losses, while $\tilde{X}_N$ equals total individual losses.

Making the appropriate substitutions from equations (4.29) through (4.32) in equation (4.19) yields

$$0 = \left(\sum_h \lambda_h^{-1}\right)\bar{R}_i - \left(\sum_h \theta_h\right) + 2\operatorname{cov}\left(R_i, \sum_{hi} v_{hi}R_i + Y_I \right.$$
$$\left. + R_N - L_N - X_N + X_I + L_I\right) \tag{4.33}$$

Using the definition of $\tilde{Y}_I$ given in equation (4.29) allows equation (4.33) to be written as

$$0 = \left(\sum_h \lambda_h^{-1}\right)\bar{R}_i - \left(\sum_h \theta_h\right)V_i + 2\,\mathrm{cov}(R_i,R_M + R_N - L_N - X_N) \quad (4.34)$$

where the total stock market value $\tilde{R}_M$ is given by

$$\tilde{R}_M = \sum_{hi} v_{hi}\tilde{R}_i + \sum_{fi} v_{fi}\tilde{R}_i \quad (4.35)$$

Since the insurance shares must be held by someone in the economy, the insurance market does not affect the price of a share in technology (i.e., stock ownership). While the nonmarket risks $\tilde{L}_N$ and $\tilde{X}_N$ do affect prices, this effect would occur in the absence of an insurance system.

The procedure used on equation (4.19) to isolate the economy-wide risks can also be used on equations (4.20), (4.21), and (4.22). The aggregated first-order conditions are

$$0 = \left(\sum_h \lambda_h^{-1}\right)\bar{Y}_f - \left(\sum_h \theta_h\right)S_f + 2\,\mathrm{cov}(Y_f,R_M + R_N - L_N - X_N) \quad (4.36)$$

$$0 = \left(\sum_h \lambda_h^{-1}\right)(\bar{R}_k - \bar{L}_k - \bar{X}_k) - \left(\sum_h \theta_h\right)A_k + 2\,\mathrm{cov}(R_k - L_k - X_k,R_M + R_N - L_N - X_N) \quad (4.37)$$

$$0 = \left(\sum_h \lambda_h^{-1}\right)(\bar{L}_k + \bar{X}_k) - \left(\sum_h \theta_h\right)P_{fk}/c_{fk} + 2\,\mathrm{cov}(L_k + X_k,R_M + R_N - L_N - X_N) \quad (4.38)$$

The final step in the aggregation of individual demands proceeds from the definitions

$$\lambda = -2\left(\sum_h \lambda_h^{-1}\right)^{-1} \quad (4.39)$$

$$\theta = \sum_h \theta_h\left(\sum_h \lambda_h^{-1}\right)^{-1} \quad (4.40)$$

The market price of risk λ is the harmonic mean of the individual marginal rates of substitution λ_h. This definition is consistent with the results of Mossin (1969), Lintner (1971), Rubinstein (1973), and Friend and Blume (1975). The new variable θ may be interpreted as the marginal rate of substitution of consumption for savings. Transforming θ in terms of the original definitions of λ_h and θ_h—equations (4.13) and (4.14)—yields

$$\theta = \frac{\sum_h U'_c/U'_v}{\sum_h U'_\mu/U'_v} \tag{4.41}$$

As first established by Mayers (1973), θ measures the aggregate consumption-savings relationship. In the presence of a riskless asset, when $\lambda_h = \lambda$ for all h, θ assumes the simple form

$$\theta = \sum_h U'_C/U'_\mu \tag{4.42}$$

Equation (4.42) clearly represents the aggregate rate of substitution of consumption for savings.

Dividing equation (4.34) and equations (4.36) through (4.38) by $(\Sigma_h \lambda_h^{-1})$ yields the system

$$0 = \bar{R}_i - \theta V_i - \lambda \operatorname{cov}(R_i, R_M + R_N - L_N - X_N) \tag{4.43}$$

$$0 = \bar{Y}_f - \theta S_f - \lambda \operatorname{cov}(Y_f, R_M + R_N - L_N - X_N) \tag{4.44}$$

$$0 = (\bar{R}_k - \bar{L}_k - \bar{X}_k) - \theta A_k - \lambda \operatorname{cov}(R_k - L_k - X_k, R_M + R_N - L_N - X_N) \tag{4.45}$$

$$0 = (\bar{L}_k + \bar{X}_k) - \theta(P_{fk}/c_{fk}) - \lambda \operatorname{cov}(L_k + X_k, R_M + R_N - L_N - X_N) \tag{4.46}$$

This set of equilibrium returns has the familiar form of the CAPM and its extensions. Individual asset returns equal a base return plus a risk premium. It is in the definition of the risk premium that the present model diverges from the CAPM tradition. Equations (4.43) through (4.46) indicate that the individual risks $\tilde{X}_{hk}$ are not removed by the insurance market. Prices of all assets are affected by both the total social risks and total individual risks.

In contrast, throughout much of the literature of financial economics, the insurance market, when present at all, is treated as a simple adjunct to the existing stock market. Insurance policies or shares are not separately accounted for in standard stock market models.[6] Yet, the results of this section indicate that an insurance market cannot be trivially adjoined to a stock market. To further explore this contention, the equilibrium system consisting of equations (4.43) through (4.46) is refined and analyzed in the next three sections to discover the properties of equilibrium insurance demands in a competitive economy.

Equilibrium Pricing Equations

The system of equations (4.43) through (4.46) describes the set of returns and prices that will prevail in a competitive equilibrium. This system has the following attributes: (1) the current value of each asset is the discounted value of the certainty equivalent of the cash flows accruing to that asset; and (2) the prices prevailing in the markets for stocks, real assets, and insurance are directly influenced by the total individual risk of the economy at large.

Writing the system of equations (4.43) through (4.46) in terms of initial prices generates the pricing equations.

$$V_i = \frac{1}{\theta}\{\bar{R}_i - \lambda \operatorname{cov}(R_i, R_M + R_N - L_N - X_N)\} \tag{4.47}$$

$$S_f = \frac{1}{\theta}\{\bar{Y}_f - \lambda \operatorname{cov}(Y_f, R_M + R_N - L_N - X_N)\} \tag{4.48}$$

$$\begin{aligned} A_k = \frac{1}{\theta}\{\bar{R}_k - \bar{L}_k - \bar{X}_k \\ - \lambda \operatorname{cov}(R_k - L_k - X_k, R_M + R_N - L_N - X_N)\} \end{aligned} \tag{4.49}$$

$$\frac{P_{fk}}{c_{fk}} = \frac{1}{\theta}\{\bar{L}_k + \bar{X}_k - \lambda \operatorname{cov}(L_k + X_k, R_M + R_N - L_N - X_N)\} \tag{4.50}$$

Equations (4.49) and (4.50) provide an interesting result when added. They indicate that fully insured real assets are priced identically to securities. Namely,

$$A_k + P_{fk}/c_{fk} = \frac{1}{\theta}\{\bar{R}_k - \lambda \operatorname{cov}(R_k, R_M + R_N - L_N - X_N)\} \tag{4.51}$$

Since the asset is fully insured, its price is independent of any specific losses. The price of an asset which is not fully insured depends upon the covariance between the social and individual risks of that asset and the risks of all other assets. This result is quite general and requires no assumptions about the independence of individual risks.

In general, the model implies that all assets are priced according to the following expression:

$$A = \frac{1}{\theta}\{\bar{A} - \lambda \operatorname{cov}(\tilde{A}, \tilde{M})\} \tag{4.52}$$

where

A = initial value of the asset
$\tilde{A}$ = terminal value of the asset with expected value A
$\tilde{M}$ = terminal value of the total market portfolio (real assets plus shares in productive firms and insurance companies)

This is a familiar asset pricing result. As long as individuals can insure their real-asset risks, all assets are priced by the same mechanism.

Thus, a generalization of the work of Mayers (1972, 1973) to include insurance results represents a return to the original asset pricing framework of Sharpe (1964). However, because of differences in initial endowments and individual risks, strong separation properties cannot be found. Even though individuals hold portfolios of stocks, real assets, insurance shares, and policies, these portfolios need not be identical in proportions among the four asset types nor within an asset type.

Importance of Individual Risks

Unlike the unsystematic errors or noise of portfolio theory, the individual risks $\tilde{X}_{hk}$ have positive means. While they may possibly be independent of other economic variables, they cannot be eliminated by naive diversification or insurance schemes. These individual risks affect the prices of real assets and insurance policies although in opposite directions. Furthermore, they increase the risk of insurance firm cash flows.

To examine these characteristics of the model more carefully and to link the model explicitly to the previous individual risk literature, assume that the individual risks $\tilde{X}_{hk}$ are independent across all individuals and asset types.[7] Using this assumption, it is straightforward but tedious to show that the system of equations (4.47) through (4.50) can be written as

$$V_i = \frac{1}{\theta}\{\bar{R}_i - \lambda\,\mathrm{cov}(R_i, R_M + R_N - L_N)\} \tag{4.53}$$

$$S_f = \frac{1}{\theta}\{\bar{Y}_f - \lambda[\mathrm{cov}(Y_f, R_M + R_N - L_N) + \xi_f \nu_H]\} \tag{4.54}$$

$$A_k = \frac{1}{\theta}\{\bar{R}_k - \bar{L}_k - \bar{X}_k - \lambda[\mathrm{cov}(R_k - L_k, R_M + R_N - L_N) + \xi_k \nu_k]\} \tag{4.55}$$

$$\frac{P_{fk}}{c_{fk}} = \frac{1}{\theta}\{\bar{L}_k - \bar{X}_k - \lambda[\mathrm{cov}(L_k, R_M + R_N - L_N) - \xi_k \nu_k]\} \tag{4.56}$$

where the measures of residual individual risk ξ_k and ξ_f are defined as

$$\xi_k \equiv \sum_h \left[a_{hk} - \sum_f n_{hfk} c_{fk} \left(1 - \frac{s_{hf}}{s_f}\right)\right] \frac{\nu_{hk}}{\nu_k} \tag{4.57}$$

$$\xi_k \equiv \frac{1}{s_f} \sum_{hk} a_{hk} n_{hfk} c_{fk} \nu_{hk} / \nu_H \tag{4.58}$$

The average individual risk ν_k is the average of the individual variances ν_{hk} of the risks $\bar{X}_{hk}$, or

$$\nu_k = \sum_h \nu_{hk}/H \tag{4.59}$$

and the total individual risk ν_H is given by

$$\nu_H = \sum_k \nu_K \tag{4.60}$$

The total shares of firm f are given by

$$s_f = \sum_h s_{hf} \tag{4.61}$$

Consistent with the previous results, the addition of equations (4.55) and (4.56) provides a standard asset pricing result independent of individual risks. This relation is intuitive. If individual risks are independent, the prices of fully insured assets should not be dependent on the individual risks.

However, some individuals must bear these risks since they are not unsystematic in the sense of having zero means. Examination of equation (4.54) reveals that the shareholders have in fact borne these risks in total. In equation (4.54), the risk of an insurance share is $\xi_f \nu_H$ as defined by equations (4.58) and (4.60). Increases in the amount of real assets a_{hk} or in the effective amount of insurance $n_{hfk} c_{fk}$ increase the residual risk priced by the market.[8] More importantly, an increase in the number of shares s_f decreases this risk.

Suppose one interprets the existing stock of real assets as a fixed risk. The definition in equation (4.58) suggests that this fixed risk is being divided into many pieces by s_f. As in Arrow and Lind (1970), subdividing a fixed risk leads to the result that no individual bears a significant fraction of the fixed risk. Unfortunately, the Arrow and Lind (1970) analogy is not complete. At the same time that an increase in insurance shares reduces the aggregate individual risk, an increase in insurance purchasing would augment that risk.

For simplicity, assume that there are H individuals in the economy with K real asset types and N assets of each type. Assume also that the ownership of these assets is uniformly distributed across the economy. Each individual owns N/H assets of each type and NK/H total real assets. Again for simplicity, assume that each individual purchases one share in each of the F insurance companies and fully insures his real assets at the same time. Let the individual variances $\nu_{hk} = \nu$ for all h and k. The total residual risk $\xi_f \nu_H$ would be

$$\xi_f \nu_H = \frac{1}{FH}[HK(N/H)^2]\nu = \frac{KN^2\nu}{FH^2} \tag{4.62}$$

Clearly, the residual risk $\xi_f \nu_H$ need not be small even if there is a large number of companies. The crucial determinant of the importance of residual risk is the size of the economy's population (FH^2) relative to its stock of assets (KN^2). As soon as life insurance is admitted into the economy, (4.62) cannot decline as the population grows since N and H will grow equally fast.

These results confirm the work of Cummins (1974) and Turner (1981) on individual risks in large markets. The assertion was advanced in these papers that the assemblage of a "large enough" pool was insufficient to guarantee the disappearance of individual risks. As the size of the pool increases, aggregate individual risks also grow. Equation (4.62) demonstrates this point. Simply increasing the size of the market does not, in general, eliminate individual risk. Yet, as in Arrow and Lind (1970), if the size of the insurance system can be increased relative to the stock of real assets, the effects of individual risks must diminish. Thus, the establishment of an insurance system leads to an immediate reduction in individual risk (or, at least in its effect, since the $\tilde{X}_{hk}$ are always present).

The residual presence of individual risk is also apparent in equations (4.55) and (4.56). The residual risk of asset k is defined as $\xi_k \nu_k$, reproduced from equations (4.57) and (4.59) as

$$\xi_k = \sum_h \left[a_{hk} - \sum_f n_{hfk} c_{fk} \left(1 - \frac{s_{hf}}{s_f}\right)\right] \nu_{hk}/\nu_k \tag{4.63}$$

Inspection of equation (4.63) reveals that $\xi_k \geqslant 0$ for any level of real assets and insurance. Since the fraction of insurance shares (s_{hf}/s_f) held by any individual must always be less than or equal to one, and since no insurance company will sell policies such that an asset is insured for more than its value ($\Sigma_f n_{hfk} c_{fk} \ngtr a_{hk}$), ξ_k must be positive (or zero).

As insurance companies become widely held, s_{hf}/s_f falls, driving ξ_k

toward zero. If each individual held an infinitesimal fraction of each insurance company and fully insured each asset, ξ_k would be driven to zero. Each asset would then be uninfluenced by individual risks.[9] As long as individuals purchase less than full insurance, individual risks remain in the pricing equations. Thus, the presence of these risks is not primarily linked to a feedback phenomenon caused by owning shares in firms that simultaneously insure the same individual's real assets. This can be seen by setting $s_{hf} = 0$ in equation (4.63). For any other individual holdings, $\xi_k > 0$ and ξ_k may be relatively large.

In the pricing equations (4.55) and (4.56), the residual individual risk $\xi_k \nu_k$ has opposite effects. Increases in residual risk increase the total risk of real assets, reducing their value. Asset types that possess inherently less residual risk are more valuable than those with more residual risk. In the absence of insurance markets, this makes intuitive sense. The variable ξ_k shows the mitigating effect of insurance markets on residual risk. On the other hand, in equation (4.56), ξ_k reduces the risk of insurance policies, increasing their value. The fewer the number of insurance policies, the larger ξ_k becomes. In an insurance equilibrium with few policies, each adjusted premium (P_{fk}/c_{fk}) would be high. An equilibirum in a well-developed insurance market would see lower policy prices presumably because the residual risks have been more evenly spread throughout the economy.[10]

These relationships seem intuitive. Without a developed insurance mechanism, real-asset owners must bear the residual, individual risk themselves. Each owner and potential owner will recognize this by placing low bids on real assets. Conversely, premiums will be high since the residual risks are not being distributed through the economy. Simply stated, insurance under these conditions is so risky that premiums must be high. Alternatively, in a developed market, since real-asset holders may purchase insurance to mitigate individual risks, real-asset prices should be high. Similarly, a greater degree of risk sharing reduces policy prices. In fact, changes in risk sharing result in dollar for dollar exchanges between asset prices A_k and the adjusted premiums P_{fk}/c_{fk}.[11]

Conclusion

In an extension of the work of Mayers (1972, 1973), this paper develops a theory of insurance markets in response to real-asset risks. Once insurance is added to the general economy, the value of any asset is the present value of the certainty-equivalent cash flows on the asset. However, this does not imply that the price mechanism is independent of individual risks. In fact, for very generally defined individual risks (i.e., not necessarily independent), the individual risks in the economy are involved in pricing every asset.

For the special case of independent individual risks, which forms the basis for most of the previous literature, the main results are preserved. Namely, individual risks affect the pricing of real assets and insurance policies in opposite directions and insurance firm shareholders are the ultimate bearers of these risks. Both in general and for independent individual risks, fully insured asset values are independent of individual risks. Nevertheless, insurance firm shareholders assume these risks in the aggregate and expect adequate compensation for them. These shareholders would not price insurance policies at expected losses without a specific risk adjustment.

Notes

1. All contracts should be viewed as tentative contracts in a tatonnement process. Although actual insurance firms tend to sell policies and subsequently invest the proceeds, the insurance mechanism is being modeled here as a Walrasian process with all trades taking place only at equilibrium prices. See Beja and Hakansson (1977) for a discussion of tentative contracts.

2. Most insurance companies do not write policies such that

$$\sum_f n_{hfk} c_{fk} > a_{hk}$$

In practice, this condition is often enforced through contractual provisions preventing overpayment.

3. Since the literature on mean-variance modeling is well known, a complete discussion of each assumption would be inappropriate here.

4. The function U_h is actually a derived utility function

$$E[u_h(\tilde{W}_h, C_h)] = U_h(\mu_h, \nu_h, C_h)$$

where u_h is a von Neumann-Morgenstern utility function. For a discussion of the implications of this approach see Fama (1970, 1976) and Samuelson (1971).

5. The approach used here follows the development of Mayers (1972, 1973).

6. Often, when insurance assets are included, the models employ the assumption of a perfect insurance market (e.g., Hakansson 1969; Fischer 1973; and Richard 1975). With perfect markets, there simply is no insurance market that contains a role for insurance companies. Individuals are able to market insurance claims in the place of firms. To maintain the integrity of their conclusions, these models are forced to assume away any consideration of moral hazard.

7. This assumption corresponds to the well-known model of Malinvaud (1971) on individual risks in large markets.

8. Under certain conditions insurance companies can reduce this risk by increasing their underwriting expenditures in a given line of insurance. If the coverage ratio can be treated as output from a production function with investment in underwriting expenditures, insurance companies can alter their exposure to risk.

9. This is not the same as saying the $\xi_f v_H$ would disappear. The key distinction is between individual risks ($\xi_k v_k$) and aggregate individual risks ($\xi_f v_H$) . While the former may be quite small, the latter may be very large.

10. Since the model developed in this chapter is an equilibrium model, with all variables determined simultaneously, it is technically incorrect to assert that a lack of policies causes prices to be high. Rather, with few outstanding policies, prices are high.

11. Suppose that the residual variance v_k changes by the amount Δ_k. The change in asset prices will be

$$\Delta A_k = \frac{-1}{\theta}(\lambda \xi_k \Delta_k)$$

whereas the change in adjusted premiums will be

$$\Delta(P_{fk}) = \frac{1}{\theta}(\lambda \xi_k \Delta_k)$$

Some care must be exercised in interpreting this result. If changes in $\xi_k v_k$ are induced through changes in asset holdings a_{hk}, n_{hfk}, or s_{hf}, changes in prices will not be equal. However, the spirit of the observation will be maintained.

References

Arrow, K.J. 1971. *Essays in the Theory of Risk Bearing*. Amsterdam: North-Holland.

Arrow, K.J., and R. Lind. 1970. Uncertainty and the evaluation of public investment decisions. *American Economic Review* 60(June):364–378.

Beja, A., and N.H. Hakansson. 1977. Dynamic market processes and the rewards to Up-to-Date Information. *Journal of Finance* 32(May):291–306.

Brainard, W., and F.T. Dolbear. 1971. Social risk and financial markets. *American Economic Review* 61(May):360–370.

Cummins, J. David. 1974. Insurer's risk: A restatement. *Journal of Risk and Insurance* 41(March): 147–157.

Dreze, J., and F. Modigliani. 1972. Consumption decisions under uncertainty. *Journal of Economic Theory* 5:308–335.

Fama, E.F. 1970. Multiperiod consumption-investment decisions. *American Economic Review* 60(March): 163–174.

Fama, E.F. 1976. Multiperiod consumption-investment decisions: a correction. *American Economic Review* 66(September):723–724.

Fischer, S. 1973. A life cycle model of life insurance purchases. *International Economic Review* 14(February):132–152.

Friend, I., and M. Blume. 1975. The demand for risky assets. *American Economic Review* 65(December):900–922.

Hakansson, N.H. 1969. Optimal investment and consumption strategies under risk, an uncertain lifetime, and insurance. *International Economic Review* 10(October):443–466.

Kihlstrom, R.E., and M.V. Pauly. 1971. The role of insurance in the allocation of risk. *American Economic Review* 61(May):371–379.

Lintner, J. 1971. Expectations, mergers, and equilibrium in purely competitive securities markets. *American Economic Review* 61(May):101–111.

Malinvaud, E. 1971. The allocation of individual risks in large markets. *Journal of Economic Theory* 4(May):312–328.

Mayers, D. 1972. Nonmarketable assets and capital market equilibrium under uncertainty. In M.C. Jensen (ed.), *Studies in the Theory of Capital Markets*. New York: Praeger.

Mayers, D. 1973. Nonmarketable assets and the determination of capital assets in the absence of a riskless asset. *Journal of Business* 46(April):258–267.

Mossin, J. 1969. Security pricing and investment criteria in competitive markets. *American Economic Review* 59(December):749–756.

Richard, S.F. 1975. Optimal consumption, portfolio, and life insurance rules for an uncertain lived individual in a continuous time model. *Journal of Financial Economics* 2(June):187–203.

Rubinstein, M. 1973. Corporate financial policy in segmented securities markets. *Journal of Financial and Quantitative Analysis* 8(December):749–761.

Samuelson, P.A. 1971. Fallacy of maximizing the geometric mean in long sequences of investing or gambling. *Proceedings of the National Academy of Sciences* (October):2493–2496.

Sharpe, W.F. 1964. Capital asset prices: A theory of market equilibrium under conditions of risk. *Journal of Finance* 19(September):425–442.

Turner, A.L. 1981. *Insurance Markets and the Behavior of Competitive Insurance Firms*. Unpublished Doctoral Dissertation, University of Pennsylvania.

5 THE DETERMINATION OF FAIR PROFITS FOR THE PROPERTY-LIABILITY INSURANCE FIRM

Alan Kraus and Stephen A. Ross

Although the property-liability insurance industry has been subject to price regulation for many years, surprisingly little research has been directed at producing valuation models of a property-liability insurance firm. Although property-liability price regulation has historically involved setting minimum prices to reduce the risk of insolvency, some commissions have begun to move toward setting prices more in the spirit of public utility regulation.[1] If, in an effort to promote efficiency, the working objective of such regulation requires the determination of prices that would prevail under competition, then regulation must be founded on some model of the costs of regulated firms. Under competition with free entry, prices just cover all economic costs, including the opportunity costs of investment by suppliers of capital, and a valuation model is required to explain how the market value of the firm, and therefore the cost of capital, reacts to changes in the prices it charges. Our objective in this chapter is to provide such a framework.

A great deal of attention and controversy in discussions of property-

---

Reprinted with permission from *Journal of Finance* 37(September 1982):1015–1028.

liability insurance regulation has been focused on whether and how investment income is to be considered when setting prices so as to produce a "fair" rate of return. Insurers receive investment income because, on average, premiums are received in advance of the payment of loss claims, and premium funds are invested during this lag. Early insurance regulation ignored investment income in setting rates but this situation has changed in the last two decades. Where investment income has come to be considered in the rate-setting process, it has apparently been, almost always, on an ad hoc basis without much economic rationale. There have recently appeared articles, by Fairley (1979) and Hill (1979), advancing the analysis of property-liability insurance rates, including investment income, in the framework of the Sharpe-Lintner-Mossin mean-variance capital-asset pricing model (CAPM). A particular purpose of these studies has been to apply the CAPM notions of systematic and unsystematic (diversifiable) risk to both underwriting and investment income to arrive at profit rates that reflect the systematic risk components of insurance.

The approach we take begins by treating the contract between the insurance firm and the policyholder, as a (nonmarketable) contingent claim whose payoff will be determined by random future events. The insurance firm is thus seen as selling short a bundle of risky securities (policies) and investing the proceeds of the short sales, plus contributed equity capital, in a competitive capital market. The policyholder has in effect simply purchased a security which will pay off contingent on some random event. This perspective makes the valuation problem particularly easy since what is actually done with the proceeds of the short sales in a competitive market is irrelevant to the valuation of the claims sold short. In such a market, the price of a contract is simply the value of the representative claim pattern. But the contract offered by the insurance company is not a simple loan. In particular, claims are paid in current dollars and this subjects the insurance firm to both the expected cost and risk of inflation. In its simplest form, this argument implies that changes in anticipated inflation have no effect on the fair premium if the real rate of interest is unaffected.

Our principal contribution to the study of these issues will be to develop a small dynamic model of the insurance contract and use it to deal rigorously with the effects of both timing of cash flows and uncertainty of basic economic state variables. We first develop the dynamic model in a simplified form and then proceed to incorporate more general assumptions. In order to concentrate on the implications of the dynamic behavior of cash flows and, in particular, of the influence of inflationary effects, we shall study the model in detail under certainty. After analyzing the certainty model, we extend it to a world in which basic economic factors are stochastic. We begin in section I with the simplest interesting version, a discrete time model and in section II we extend the model to a truly dynamic setting. Section III examines the one period stochastic model, akin to the Fairley (1979) and Hill (1979) analyses, and section IV develops the intertemporal stochastic model. Section V briefly concludes the paper.

I. Discrete time Certainty Model

Let us begin with the simplest possible model. We assume that each policy is priced competitively and is written for a single period, with the premium for period t, P_t, received at the beginning of the period and the loss, L_t, paid out at the end.[2] If we denote the nominal interest rate by r_t, the fair price for insurance in this certain world is given by

$$P_t = \frac{L_t}{1 + r_t} \tag{5.1}$$

Since claims are paid in nominal dollars, L_t reflects the impact of inflation over the period. If the general inflation rate is denoted by i_t and the real interest rate is denoted by ϱ_t^*, then by the Fisher equation $(1 + r_t) = (1 + \varrho_t^*)(1 + i_t)$, and if the cost of settling claims is expected to inflate at the rate π_t, then $L_t = L_{t-1}(1 + \pi_t)$. If $\pi_t = i_t$, then equation (5.1) becomes

$$P_t = \frac{L_{t-1}}{1 + \varrho_t^*} \tag{5.2}$$

If the real rate stays constant, then the equilibrium premium should rise at the actual realized inflation rate. Notice, too, that changes in anticipated inflation affect the equilibrium premium only through changes in the real rate of interest. If ϱ_t^* remains constant, then an increase in the nominal interest rate, r_t, with an increase in anticipated inflation, will have no impact on P_t provided the anticipated inflation in average losses, π_t, rises with the general inflation level.

More generally, if we allow for relative price changes between losses and other nominal quantities, then

$$\frac{P_{t+1}}{P_t} = \left[\frac{(1 + \varrho_t^*)(1 + \pi_{t+1})}{(1 + \varrho_{t+1}^*)(1 + i_{t+1})}\right](1 + i_t) \tag{5.3}$$

which implies that a wedge can be driven between premium inflation and general inflation through changes either in the real rate or in the real value of the average loss.

Actual cash flows come from combining these policies over time and accounting for changes in the stock of policies and claims. To see the extent to which our general principles carry over to a more realistic world, we shall extend the analysis to a dynamic model which is simple, but sufficiently realistic to accommodate the principal dynamic influences.

II. Dynamic Certainty Model

Our basic dynamic model is given by the following two differential equations:

$$\dot{Q}_t = S_t - \delta Q_t \tag{5.4}$$

and

$$\dot{C}_t = \alpha_t Q_t - \theta C_t \tag{5.5}$$

where Q_t denotes the stock of policies in force at time t, S_t is a function giving the current sales of new policies, δ is the rate of attrition of existing policies through nonrenewal, C_t is the stock of unsettled claims, α_t is the accident frequency, and θ is the rate of settlement. These equations say that the policy stock is augmented by new sales and declines by attrition through nonrenewals, while the stock of unsettled claims grows by the rate of accidents among outstanding policies and declines by the rate of claim settlements. By making sales an appropriate function of relative prices, this system could equally well describe a single firm within a competitive industry or the industry itself—whether competitive or not. The reasonableness of this model hinges primarily on the assumed homogeneity of claims which is a central part of our analysis. To the extent to which claims and their attendant losses are too "lumpy," the argument would have to be modified.

The above equations can describe a variety of different dynamic paths for both policies and claims depending upon the assumptions we make on the sales and accident rates. When we consider stochastic generalizations of this model, we shall permit α to vary, but in the present section we treat it as constant. Our point of view, though, permits us to allow completely general sales functions, S_t. Since, under competition, the cohort of policies sold at any time must pay for itself, sales can have no influence on pricing in our model. Consequently, we assume $S = 0$ for the following development. For simplicity, we also assume that the attrition rate, δ, is zero.[3] With these assumptions, our dynamic system consists of (5.5) alone.

Our problem is to determine the fair or competitive pricing of a given cohort of policies. For convenience, we assume this cohort of policies is issued at time $t = 0$ and offers coverage over a period of length T. For simplicity, we assume that premiums are paid in full at time of issue, but more general payment schedules, like general sales schedules, are easily accommodated by superimposing the analysis of this section; the generalizations are straightforward. For convenience of notation, we set $Q_0 = 1$, so that the cohort consists of a single policy and P_0 is the revenue collected at time 0. Since this policy is issued at time 0, $C_0 = 0$.

Solving (5.5) for the stock of claims at time t, we have

$$C_t = \begin{cases} \dfrac{\alpha}{\theta}(1 - e^{-\theta t}) & \text{for} \quad 0 \leqslant t \leqslant T \\ \dfrac{\alpha}{\theta}(1 - e^{-\theta T})e^{-\theta(t-T)} & \text{for} \quad t > T \end{cases} \tag{5.6}$$

where the break at T occurs because no new claims are generated against these policies after the coverage period, T. (In effect, $\alpha_t = 0$ for $t > T$.)

If we denote the price index for the average claim by q_t and assume that it grows at the exponential rate π, then

$$q_t = q_0 e^{\pi t} \tag{5.7}$$

It follows that the dollar cash outflows from losses are given by

$$L_t = \theta q_0 e^{\pi t} C_t \tag{5.8}$$

and the fair or competitive price for insurance, P_0, is given by the present value of these dollar losses. Letting r and ϱ denote the nominal interest rate and the real rate of return on policies, respectively, where $\varrho \equiv r - \pi$, we have

$$\begin{aligned} P_0 &= \int_0^{\infty} L_t e^{-rt}\, dt \\ &= q_0 \alpha \left(\frac{\theta}{\varrho + \theta}\right)\left(\frac{1 - e^{-\varrho T}}{\varrho}\right) \end{aligned} \tag{5.9}$$

and

$$P_0 \approx (\alpha T) q_0 \left(\frac{\theta}{\varrho + \theta}\right)\left(1 - \frac{1}{2}(\varrho T)\right) \tag{5.10}$$

where the approximation is derived by simple Taylor series expansion. Notice that our previous simple results on the impact of realized inflation and changes in anticipated inflation remain valid. If the real rate of interest is unaltered by changes in the anticipated inflation rate of losses, then premiums should not change. As expected, premiums must rise if the rate of claim settlement, θ, is increased.[4] Similarly, premiums should rise with the price level, q_0.[5] Of course, we have defined the real rate of return on policies by subtracting the nominal inflation rate on losses rather than the economy-wide inflation rate. If i denotes the economy-wide rate and ϱ^* denotes the real rate of interest for the economy, then $\varrho = \varrho^* - (\pi - i)$, and the differences between ϱ and ϱ^* can be seen to arise from differences in the two inflation rates. With ϱ^* constant, if π and i move together, then changes in the nominal rate of interest will leave premiums unaffected.

An important book quantity in the insurance industry, and in its regulation, is the rate of underwriting profit, or underwriting margin, defined as the ratio of the difference between premium income and total undiscounted dollar losses to premium income. To examine underwriting margin in our model, we first calculate total undiscounted dollar losses:

$$\begin{aligned} UDL &\equiv \int_0^\infty L_t dt \\ &= q_0\alpha\left(\frac{\theta}{\theta - \pi}\right)\left(\frac{e^{\pi T} - 1}{\pi}\right) \end{aligned} \tag{5.11}$$

where we assume $\pi < \theta$.

The underwriting margin is given by

$$\begin{aligned} U_0 &\equiv \frac{P_0 - UDL}{P_0} \\ &= 1 - \frac{\left(\frac{\theta}{\theta - \pi}\right)\left(\frac{e^{\pi T} - 1}{\pi}\right)}{\left(\frac{\theta}{\theta + \varrho}\right)\left(\frac{1 - e^{\varrho T}}{\varrho}\right)} \\ &\approx -\left(\frac{r}{\theta - \pi}\right)\left(1 + \frac{1}{2}(\theta + \varrho)T\right) \end{aligned} \tag{5.12}$$

Following Fairley (1979, pp. 196–198), if we let k be defined as the investable funds per dollar of premiums, the $U_0 = -kr$ implies

$$k \approx \frac{1 + \frac{1}{2}(\theta + \varrho)T}{\theta - \pi} \tag{5.13}$$

Notice that k is a decreasing function of the settlement rate, θ, and an increasing function of the inflation rate, π. Keeping realistic magnitudes in mind, if we take the average delay in claims, $1/\theta$, to be about one year it will dominate inflation and the real rate in determining k, which will be approximately 1.5. Intuitively, raising the claim delay should increase the investable funds per dollar of premiums, and equation (5.13) verifies this result.

The fact that k increases with inflation—even if the nominal rate is held constant and ϱ adjusts—is a bit more difficult to fathom. The easiest way to see this result is to recall that as the inflation rate is increased the fair premium stays constant, but the summed losses rise, becoming infinite as the inflation rate approaches the claim settlement rate. As a consequence, the underwriting profit becomes arbitrarily negative. Even if the real rate approaches zero for high inflation rates, the premium is still bounded above by the expected loss, $\alpha T q_t$.[6]

Before we close this section, we should reiterate that the above results apply to quite general sales and claim dynamics. In addition, sales costs, claim expenses, and the like can be easily analyzed, usually by just adjusting the price index and the premium to make them gross of such costs.

We turn now to the situation where losses are stochastic in the aggregate.

III. Single Period Stochastic Model

In introducing uncertainty into our model, we emphasize that it is not actuarial risk that will concern us. By assumption, the firm we consider is large enough for individual actuarial risks to even out in the aggregate. It is only the risk of the firm's aggregate cash flow that matters to suppliers of capital, and only the systematic component of that risk (the portion that is not diversifiable across different firms) that affects the market value of the firm.

It is easiest to study the stochastic case first in a single-period world (in which we suppress the time subscript for convenience). Applying the Arbitrage Pricing Theory of Ross (1976, 1977), we find the competitive premium by considering the covariances of the loss, $\tilde{L}$, with the systematic risk factors which are priced in the economy, $(x_1, \ldots, x_n)$. This risk correction gives

$$P = \frac{E[\tilde{L}] - \sum_i \lambda_i[\text{cov}(\tilde{L},\tilde{x}_i)/\text{var}(\tilde{x}_i)]}{1 + r}$$

where $\tilde{x}_i$ is the ith systematic risk factor and λ_i is the price of the ith component of risk. Letting β_i^L be the regression coefficient of the loss of $\tilde{x}_i$, we have

$$P = \frac{E[\tilde{L}] - \sum_i \lambda_i \beta_i^L}{1 + r}$$

Specializing to the CAPM model of Sharpe (1964) and Lintner (1965) yields

$$P = \frac{E[\tilde{L}] - \lambda\beta^L}{1 + r}$$

where

$$\beta^L \equiv \frac{\operatorname{cov}(\tilde{L}, \tilde{R}_m)}{\operatorname{var}(\tilde{R}_m)}$$

is the regression coefficient of the loss on the market return, $\tilde{R}_m$, and

$$\lambda \equiv (E_m - r)$$

is the excess return on the market.

In other words, we alter the certainty theory by correcting for the risk premium. Notice that if, as empirical estimates suggest, the beta coefficient on losses is negative, then this will raise the fair premium above its value under certainty.[7]

If the beta coefficient is redefined as the beta coefficient of losses per premium dollar, that is,

$$\beta_L \equiv \frac{\operatorname{cov}\left(\frac{\tilde{L}}{P}, \tilde{R}_m\right)}{\operatorname{var}(\tilde{R}_m)}$$

then the expected underwriting profit is

$$U \equiv \frac{P - E[\tilde{L}]}{P} = -[r + (E_m - r)\beta_L]$$

which is Fairley's and Hill's estimate of the fair profit rate.[8] (Equivalently, we could also define β_L as the negative of the regression coefficient of underwriting profits on the market portfolio; since premiums are given, this will lead to the same analysis.)

Notice that if β_L is constant, the above formulas produce precisely the same inflation corrections as before. Premiums rise with the dollar value of losses and are not affected by changes in anticipated inflation. To put it somewhat more directly, β^L rises proportionately with the price level for losses, and changes in the anticipated inflation rate are offset by equal changes in the nominal interest rate. We shall study these issues in greater detail in the stochastic intertemporal setting below.

IV. Intertemporal Stochastic Model

Assume, as above in the single period case, that systematic, economy-wide risk is completely described by a state vector $x \equiv (x_1, \ldots, x_n)$. The vector x impounds all exogenous activity affecting the basic economic variables of our system. Knowledge of this vector is sufficient to determine the distribution of future returns. Each of the factors is priced in the market place, resulting in an equilibrium in which the expected excess return (above the riskless rate) on any asset is linearly related to the covariances of the asset's return with these factors. A detailed derivation of these arguments is given in Ross (1976) and Cox, Ingersoll, and Ross (1980). To apply this equilibium relation to our situation, we require some further specification and assumptions.

We shall assume that the state vector x is multivariate lognormal, so that its movement in continuous time is described by

$$d\tilde{x}_i = m_i x_i \, dt + \sigma_i x_i \, d\tilde{z}_i \qquad i = 1, \ldots, n \tag{5.14}$$

where m_i and σ_i are intertemporal constants, and $d\tilde{z} \equiv (d\tilde{z}_1, \ldots, d\tilde{z}_n)$ is a multivariate independent Wiener process.

Define $V = V(x,C,t)$ as the value at time t of the remaining cash outflows from claim settlements on a single policy (i.e., for $Q_t = 1$) when the state vector is x and the unsettled claims against the policy are C at time t. As before, we assume that the policy under consideration is issued at time $t = 0$ and offers coverage up to time T. Hence the fair premium is given by $P_0 = V(x,0,0)$, the value when the policy is written.

We complete our specification of the model by assuming that the dynamic system of section II still governs the claim flow, with both the accident frequency and the price level of claims as functions of the state variables. We parametrize these as

$$\log \alpha = \sum_i \alpha_i \log x_i + \log \alpha_0 \tag{5.15}$$

and

$$\log q = \sum_i q_i \log x_i + \log q_0 \tag{5.16}$$

The loglinear functions assumed above are general enough to permit econometric estimation, but simple enough to lend themselves to an analytic solution.

The application to our model of the basic equilibrium relation that the expected excess return on an asset is linearly related to the covariances of its return with the underlying factor gives

$$E\left[\frac{d\tilde{V}}{V}\right] + \left[\frac{\theta qC}{V} - r\right] dt = \sum_i \lambda_i \sigma_i \left[\operatorname{cov}\left(\frac{d\tilde{V}}{V}, \frac{d\tilde{x}_i}{x_i}\right) \Big/ \operatorname{var}\left(\frac{d\tilde{x}_i}{x_i}\right)\right] dt \tag{5.17}$$

where $\lambda_1, \ldots, \lambda_n$ are constants.[9] Claim settlements, θqC, are analogous to dividend payouts on a stock and thus are part of the total return. The right-hand terms in square brackets are the beta coefficients of the return on the asset with respect to each of the factors. For the special case of the traditional CAPM, only the beta with respect to the single factor of return on the market would be included.

Applying Ito's Lemma to the value of remaining cash outflows and using the dynamic system assumed, we obtain

$$\begin{aligned} d\tilde{V} &= \sum_i V_i d\tilde{x}_i + V_c dC + V_t dt + \frac{1}{2}\sum_i V_{ii}(d\tilde{x}_i)^2 \\ &= \sum_i V_i(m_i x_i dt + \sigma_i x_i d\tilde{z}_i) + \frac{1}{2}\sum_i V_{ii}\sigma_i^2 x_i^2 dt \\ &\quad + V_c(\alpha - \theta C)dt + V_t dt \end{aligned} \tag{5.18}$$

where V_i, V_{ii}, V_C, and V_t denote partial derivatives. Using the equilibrium relation (5.17), the basic valuation equation becomes[10]

$$\begin{aligned} &\frac{1}{2}\sum_i \sigma_i^2 x_i^2 V_{ii} + \sum_i (m_i - \lambda_i\sigma_i)x_i V_i + (\alpha - \theta C)V_c \\ &\qquad + V_t - rV + \theta qC = 0 \qquad \text{for } t \leqslant T \end{aligned} \tag{5.19}$$

and

$$\begin{aligned} &\frac{1}{2}\sum_i \sigma_i^2 x_i^2 V_{ii} + \sum_i (m_i - \lambda_i\sigma_i)x_i V_i - \theta C V_c \\ &\qquad + V_t - rV + \theta qC = 0 \qquad \text{for } t > T \end{aligned} \tag{5.20}$$

To solve this system for the fair premium, it is easiest to separate it into two parts. After the coverage period, that is, $t > T$, the value will be independent of calendar time and depends only upon x and the stock of unsettled claims, C. The dynamic pricing equation (5.20) is separable in x and C. It is intuitively clear that the value must be linearly homogeneous in C and must have a solution of the form $v(x,C) = g(x)C$.

Substituting this into (5.20) yields

$$\frac{1}{2}\sum_i \sigma_i^2 x_i^2 g_{ii} + \sum_i (m_i - \lambda_i\sigma_i)x_i g_i - (r + \theta)g + \theta q = 0 \tag{5.21}$$

and solving we obtain

$$g(x) = g_0 \prod_i x_i^{q_i} + \text{complementary solution} \tag{5.22}$$

where

$$g_0 \equiv -\theta q_0\left[\frac{1}{2}\sum_i \sigma_i^2 q_i(q_i - 1) + \sum_i (m_i - \lambda_i\sigma_i)q_i - (r + \theta)\right]^{-1} \tag{5.23}$$

We discard the complementary solution (to the homogeneous equation) by considering the value of remaining cash outflows in the case of zero inflation (i.e., $q_i = 0$ for all i).[11]

Our task now is to relate this solution to the solution in the region where policies are still liable for new claims: $t \in [0,T]$. Clearly the stock of existing claims at time t, C, is "sunk" in economic terms, and may be separated from the value of claims yet to be filed. Hence, we may write

$$V(x,C,t) = v(x,C) + h(x,t) \tag{5.24}$$

where $h(x,t)$ denotes the value attached to remaining claims to be filed from t to T (and is independent of C since new claims arise independently of claims already filed). This latter, value, in a risk neutral world, would simply be the discounted expected value of the future claims. In a world with risk premia, it is still the discounted expected value, but with the state variables assumed to move at a drift rate that is net of the risk premia (see Cox, Ingersoll, and Ross 1980). The cost of a marginal increment to the claim stock, $v_c(x,C)$, is simply $g(x)$. Since accidents occur at the rate α, we have, using equations (5.15) and (5.16),

$$h(x,t) = \left[E\int_t^T \alpha(x_\tau)v_c(x_\tau,0)e^{-r(\tau-t)}\,d\tau\right]$$

subject to

$$d\tilde{x} = (\mathrm{m} - \lambda\sigma)x\,dt + \sigma x\,d\tilde{z}$$

$$= \alpha_0 g_0 E\left[\int_t^T \prod_i (x_i)^{\alpha_i} \prod_i (x_i)^{q_i} e^{-r(\tau-t)}\, d\tau\right]$$

$$h(x,t) = \alpha g\left[\sum_i [(m_i - \lambda_i\sigma_i)(q_i + \alpha_i) + \frac{1}{2}\sigma_i^2(q_i + \alpha_i)(q_i + \alpha_i - 1)] - r\right]^{-1}$$

$$- r^{-1} \times \left\{\exp\left[\left(\sum_i [(m_i - \lambda_i\sigma_i)(q_i + \alpha_i)\right.\right.\right.$$

$$\left.\left.\left. + \frac{1}{2}\sigma_i^2(q_i + \alpha_i)(q_i + \alpha_i - 1)] - r\right)(T - t)\right] - 1\right\} \tag{5.25}$$

Hence, at $t = 0$, we have for the fair premium, using (5.16), (5.22), and (5.23),

$$P_0 = V(x,0,0) = v(x,0) + h(x,0) = g(x) \times 0 + h(x,0) = h(x,0)$$

$$= \theta\alpha q\left[\sum_i [(m_i - \lambda_i\sigma_i)(q_i + \alpha_i)\right.$$

$$\left. + \frac{1}{2}\sigma_i^2(q_i + \alpha_i)(q_i + \alpha_i - 1)] - r\right]^{-1}$$

$$\times \left[(r + \theta) - \frac{1}{2}\sum_i \sigma_i^2 q_i(q_i - 1) - \sum_i (m_i - \lambda_i\sigma_i)q_i\right]^{-1}$$

$$\times \left\{\exp\left[\left(\sum_i [(m_i - \lambda_i\sigma_i)(q_i + \alpha_i)\right.\right.\right.$$

$$\left.\left.\left. + \frac{1}{2}\sigma_i^2(q_i + \alpha_i)(q_i + \alpha_i - 1)] - r\right) T\right] - 1\right\} \tag{5.26}$$

As a check on our result, notice that if there is no uncertainty ($\sigma_i = 0$ for all i), the accident rate is constant ($\Sigma_i m_i \alpha_i = 0$), and the inflation rate is $\pi = \Sigma_i m_i q_i$ then (5.26) yields

$$P_0 = \frac{\theta\alpha_0 q_0}{(\varrho + \theta)}\left[\frac{1 - e^{-\varrho T}}{\varrho}\right]$$

as we had before in equation (5.9).

With uncertainty, the price index for the average loss follows the diffusion.

$$\frac{d\tilde{q}}{q} = \left[\sum_i \left(\frac{1}{2}\sigma_i^2 q_i(q_i - 1) + q_i m_i\right)\right] dt + \sum_i q_i\sigma_i\, d\tilde{z}_i$$

$$\equiv \pi \, dt + \sigma_q \, d\tilde{z}_q \tag{5.27}$$

where π is the expected inflation rate for losses.

If we define the dollar frequency rate for accidents as $l = \alpha q$, then

$$\frac{d\tilde{l}}{l} = \left[\sum_i \left(\frac{1}{2}\sigma_i^2(\alpha_i + q_i)(\alpha_i + q_i - 1) + (\alpha_i + q_i)m_i\right)\right] dt$$

$$+ \sum_i (\alpha_i + q_i)\sigma_i \, d\tilde{z}$$

$$\equiv \pi_\alpha \, dt + \sigma_\alpha \, d\tilde{z}_\alpha \tag{5.28}$$

Substituting (5.27) and (5.28) into (5.26) we obtain a remarkably simple expression analogous to the result for the riskless case (5.9).

$$P_0 = \left(\frac{\theta \alpha q}{\varrho + \theta}\right)\left[\frac{1 - e^{-\varrho_\alpha T}}{\varrho_\alpha}\right] \tag{5.29}$$

where

$$\varrho \equiv r - \pi + \sum_i \lambda_i \sigma_i q_i$$

and

$$\varrho_\alpha \equiv r - \pi_\alpha + \sum_i \lambda_i \sigma_i (q_i + \alpha_i)$$

are risk adjusted real rates.

We can now verify that our previous analysis of the influence of past and anticipated inflation carries over to the uncertain world. If the inflation rate, π, increases and real rates remain unaltered, then the competitive premium is unaltered. Similarly, if the real accident frequency is unaffected by the price level, then the premium will rise with the price level. In the special case when $\alpha_i = 0$ (the accident frequency is held constant), we have $\varrho_\alpha = \varrho$.

What, then is the influence of risk on the competitive premium? It is easiest to see the comparison with the single period beta effect by simplifying our assumptions.

Suppose that there is only one source of uncertainty, x_1, which influences inflation and the accident rate and which is priced in the market place—that is, for which $\lambda_1 > 0$. For comparison purposes, $d\tilde{x}_1/x_1$ could be the return on the market portfolio. Now, the risk premia for inflation and losses are of the form $\lambda_1\sigma_1 q_1$, and $\lambda_1\sigma_1(q_1 + \alpha_1)$, respectively. From (5.27) and (5.28) we have that

$$\beta_q \equiv \frac{\operatorname{cov}\left(\dfrac{d\tilde{q}}{q}, \dfrac{d\tilde{x}_1}{x_1}\right)}{\operatorname{var}\left(\dfrac{d\tilde{x}_1}{x_1}\right)} = q_1 \tag{5.30}$$

and

$$\beta_l \equiv \frac{\operatorname{cov}\left(\dfrac{d\tilde{l}}{l}, \dfrac{d\tilde{x}_1}{x_1}\right)}{\operatorname{var}\left(\dfrac{d\tilde{x}_1}{x_1}\right)} = \alpha_1 + q_1 \tag{5.31}$$

Hence, letting $\lambda_1 = (E_m - r)/\sigma_1$, we have

$$\varrho = r - \tau + (E_m - r)\beta_q$$

and

$$\varrho_\alpha = r - \pi_\alpha + (E_m - r)\beta_l$$

Notice from (5.29) that each beta will influence the fair premium separately, and that if the betas are negative, then the risk adjustment raises the competitive premium.

It is also easy to compute the expected total undiscounted loss to get the competitive premium in terms of that loss and the resultant underwriting profit. Without discounting (i.e., $r = 0$ so $\varrho = -\pi$ and $\varrho_\alpha = -\pi_\alpha$) and with $\lambda_1 = 0$, (5.29) gives this loss,

$$\begin{aligned} UDL &\equiv E\left\{\int_0^\infty \theta q C\, dt\right\} \\ &= \left(\frac{\theta \alpha q}{\theta - \pi}\right)\left[\frac{e^{\tau_\alpha T} - 1}{\pi_\alpha}\right] \end{aligned} \tag{5.32}$$

and the underwriting profit is

$$\begin{aligned} U &= \frac{P_0 - UDL}{P_0} \\ &= 1 - \left(\frac{\varrho + \theta}{\theta - \pi}\right)\left[\frac{e^{\pi_\alpha T} - 1}{\pi_\alpha}\right]\left[\frac{1 - e^{-\varrho_\alpha T}}{\varrho_\alpha}\right]^{-1} \\ &\approx -\left(\frac{r}{\theta - \pi}\right)\left[1 + \frac{1}{2}(\theta + \varrho)T\right] \\ &\quad - \left(\frac{E_m - r}{\theta - \pi}\right)\left[\beta_q + \frac{1}{2}(\theta + \varrho)T\beta_l\right] \end{aligned} \tag{5.33}$$

where, again, approximations are by simple Taylor series expansion. This final result makes the risk adjustment to the underwriting profit transparent. If ϱ is small and if the inflation beta, β_q, together with the dollar accident beta, β_l, weighted by the average number of claims per policy is negative, then the underwriting profit will be adjusted upward along with the fair premium, above the riskless level.

V. Conclusions

To summarize our findings, we have basically shown that since the property-liability insurance contract gives payouts in nominal dollars, the competitive premium is insulated against changes in the nominal rate through changes in the anticipated inflation rate. In other words, the premium is affected by inflation only in so far as real rates of interest are impacted. Of course, over time this same analysis will imply that since competitive premia are denominated in current dollars, they will rise with inflation.

The introduction of risk means that the policyholder receives a contract whose risk-free value is modified by the betas of both the accident rate and the inflation rate. The competitive premium will vary inversely with these betas since the rate of return to the policyholder will increase as they are increased. This simply says that if insurance losses are a hedge against systematic economic risk (i.e., betas are negative) then fair premiums will be higher than discounted expected losses, thereby reflecting the increased value of the insurance contract. Further theoretical research should examine these effects with an explicitly stochastic interest rate—this would be an important extension of the present work on the impact of inflation.

Empirically testing and implementing this theory requires estimation of the claim delay, of the stochastic structure of the average accident frequency, and of the average inflation rates for losses by insurance lines. These can then be used to determine the relationship between actual premiums and market determined premiums, and among other uses, they would provide a test of the competitive structure of the industry.

Notes

1. For example, see Hill (1979, p. 174, esp. note 6).

2. In this and in subsequent models, all expenses associated with policy sales are netted from the premium and all expenses associated with claims are included in a definition of the loss.

3. Equivalently, we can assume that when a policyholder drops coverage, the fair rebate is given. This effect is small and the rebate—even if not fair—makes it negligible.

4. We are implicitly assuming that the settlement rate is bounded from below by regulation or competition since the notion of a competitive premium is meaningless if the insurer is free to make the settlement rate as low as desired.

5. Another possibility is that the dollar value of the loss is frozen at the time of the accident. Letting C_t^* denote the dollar value of unsettled claims at time t, we have

$$\dot{C}_t^* = \alpha q_t Q_t - \theta C_t^* = \alpha q_0 e^{\pi t} - \theta C_t^*$$

which has the soluton

$$C_t^* = \left(\frac{\alpha q_0}{\theta + \pi}\right)(e^{\pi t} - e^{-\theta t}) \qquad \text{for} \quad 0 \leqslant t \leqslant T$$

$$\left(\frac{\alpha q_0}{\theta + \pi}\right)(e^{\pi T} - e^{-\theta T})e^{-\theta(t-T)} \qquad \text{for} \quad t > T$$

Thus, since $L_t = \theta C_t^*$, the present value of losses is

$$PVL = \int_0^\infty L_t e^{-rt}\,dt$$

$$= \left(\frac{\alpha\theta q_0}{\theta + \pi}\right)\left[\frac{\pi + \theta}{\varrho(r + \theta)}\right](1 - e^{-\varrho T})$$

so that the fair premium is

$$P_0 = \left(\frac{\alpha\theta q_0}{\theta + r}\right)\frac{1 - e^{-\varrho T}}{\varrho} \tag{5.10a}$$

Now, the original result on premiums rising with inflation remains unaltered, but an increase in anticipated inflation will lower premiums with real rates unaltered. The reason is simply that higher nominal rates accelerate the discounting of claims awaiting settlement.

As a practical matter, though, increases in nominal interest rates from increases in inflation would have a very small impact on premia, since, for $\theta = 1.5$ and $r = 0.1$, for example,

$$\frac{r}{P}\frac{\partial P}{\partial r} = \frac{r}{\theta + r} = -0.06$$

Raising r to 0.15, a 50% increase, would lower premiums by only 3%.

In general, we would expect some portion of costs from an accident at time t to continue to inflate while a portion remained fixed. We could model this by reinterpreting r as the nominal rate minus the average inflation rate on costs past the accident. Alternatively, if γ is that proportion subject to inflation at the rate π and $(1 - \gamma)$ is, as above, not affected by inflation, then the fair premium would be a weighted average of (5.10) and (5.10a):

$$P_0 = \alpha\theta q_0\left[\frac{1 - e^{-\varrho T}}{\varrho}\right]\left[\gamma\left(\frac{1}{\theta + \varrho}\right) + (1 - \gamma)\left(\frac{1}{\theta + r}\right)\right]$$

More generally, the latter term would be an average over different inflation rates for different components.

As we have seen, though, none of these modifications alters the dynamic behavior of premia and the magnitude of the influence of changing anticipated inflation rates would be small.

6. As a practical matter, if the evidence on very low real rates (see Fama 1975 and Fama and Schwert 1979) applies to the insurance sector, then the fair premium will be set at the expected loss, despite the fact that premiums are "loaned" by policyholders ahead of loss receipts.

7. See Hill (1979, p. 185) and Fairley (1979, p. 204).

8. For example, see Fairley (1979, p. 201).

9. Cox, Ingersoll, and Ross (1980) provide a derivation of this basic equilibrium model.

10. We shall assume, for simplicity, that r is not stochastic. The impact of stochastic interest rates is of interest, but the analysis would be complicated. We are, also, again assuming that losses continue to inflate with the price level after the coverage period. The modifications of the results of this section to the alternative case of note 5 can be easily applied to this case.

11. The solution to the homogeneous equation from (5.21) is

$$a_0 \Pi_i x_i^{a_i}$$

where a_0 is an arbitrary parameter and the parameters a_i must satisfy the constraint

$$\frac{1}{2}\sum_i \sigma_i^2 a_i^2 + \sum_i (m_i - \lambda_i \sigma_i - \sigma_i^2) a_i - (r + \theta) = 0$$

For $t > T$, $C_{t+s} = C_t e^{-\theta s}$, so that when $q_i = 0$ for all i in (5.16) (and, thus, $q = q_0$ with zero inflation), it follows that:

$$v(x,C) = \int_0^\infty \theta q_0 C e^{-(r+\theta)s}\, ds = \frac{\theta q_0 C}{r + \theta}$$

However, $q_i = 0$ for all i also implies $g_0 \Pi_i x_i^{q} = \dfrac{\theta q_0}{r + \theta}$ so that $v(x, C) = g(x)C$ can only be satisfied if $a_0 = 0$ in the complementary solution. For the same solution to (5.21) to govern the case of zero inflation as well as the general case, therefore, requires $a_0 = 0$, so that the complementary solution vanishes.

References

Cox, J., J. Ingersoll, and S. Ross. 1980. A theory of the term structure of interest rates. Stanford University Graduate School of Business Working Paper.

Fairley, W.B. 1979. Investment income and profit margins in property-liability insurance: Theory and empirical results. *Bell Journal of Economics* 10(Spring): 192–210.

Fama, E.F. 1975. Short-term interest rates as predictors of inflation. *American*

Economic Review 65(June): 269–282.

Fama, E.F., and G.W. Schwert. 1979. Inflation interest, and relative prices. *Journal of Business* 52(April):183–209.

Hill, R.D. 1979. Profit regulation in property-liability insurance. *Bell Journal of Economics* 10(Spring):172–191.

Lintner, J. 1965. The valuation of risk assets and the selection of risky investments in stock portfoiios and capital budgets. *Review of Economics and Statistics* 47(February):13–37.

Ross, S.A. 1976. The arbitrage theory of capital asset pricing. *Journal of Economic Theory* 13(December):341–360.

Ross, S.A. 1977. Risk, return and arbitrage. In I. Friend and J.L. Bicksler, *Risk and Return in Finance*, vol. 1. Cambridge, MA: Ballinger pp.189–218.

Sharpe, W.F. 1964. Capital asset prices: A theory of market equilibrium under conditions of risk. *Journal of Finance* 19(September):425–442.

6 THE USE OF INVESTMENT INCOME IN MASSACHUSETTS PRIVATE PASSENGER AUTOMOBILE AND WORKERS' COMPENSATION RATEMAKING

Richard A. Derrig

It seems that Massachusetts is known throughout the property-casualty insurance world for its unusual system of ratemaking. Except for a brief hiatus in 1977, private passenger automobile insurance rates have been set annually by the Commissioner of Insurance for use by all companies writing business in the Commonwealth. The workers' compensation line is regulated similarly but with an independent industry bureau making filings for rate changes. Those rate changes, however, need the prior approval of the Commissioner of Insurance before taking effect. The workers' compensation rates are also used by all companies operating in Massachusetts. This close regulation of the two major lines of property-casualty insurance is chiefly responsible for the divergence of Massachusetts ratemaking methods from those employed in the rest of the United States. This chapter reviews the development of the methodology used to establish under-

---

This chapter is an extension of a presentation to the Worker's Compensation Rating Organizations Meeting, May 11, 1983. The author gratefully acknowledges the helpful contributions of Acheson H. Callaghan, Jr., Robert F. Conger, J. David Cummins, Scott Harrington, Scott P. Lewis, and committee members of the Massachusetts Rating Bureau.

writing profit provisions for these two lines under rate regulation in Massachusetts during the period 1975–1983.

Explicit recognition of investment income in Massachusetts ratemaking was first highlighted in the initial rate decision issued by Insurance Commissioner James M. Stone in May, 1975.[1] Various methods of dealing with this issue were introduced and refined at subsequent rate hearings for automobile and workers' compensation insurance during the next eight years. Explicit methodologies were proposed by expert witnesses for the industry, the Attorney General, and the Division of Insurance. This chapter first considers the general evolution of the underwriting profit provisions used in the approved rates.[2] Separate summaries are made in the next two sections for private passenger automobile and workers' compensation rates. A survey of the key parameters and important issues concerning their measurement is presented in the fourth section. The fifth section illustrates the sensitivity of underwriting provisions to the parameters chosen, and, with the aid of the hindsight gained by 1984, compares the actual results for the two lines to the target results established by the various rate approvals. The concluding section contains a brief summary of the discussion.

Private Passenger Auto Insurance Rates

Although this section reviews automobile insurance rate decisions from 1976 to 1983, the beginning of the Massachusetts story lies in Stone's initial decision on workers' compensation rates on May 22, 1975 (Stone 1975). For those rates, the insurance industry had filed the traditional underwriting profit and contingency provision of 2.5 percent of premiums. While most other components of the ratemaking mechanism were justified by relying explicitly on recent data for premiums, losses, and expenses, the underwriting profit provision was a fixed budgetary item seemingly buttressed only by tradition. Stone's knowledge of the importance of investment income to total industry profits most likely led him to demand that the underwriting profit provision be explicitly justified as well.

The ratemaking methods Stone reviewed reflected the industry's commonly held view that investment and underwriting were separate operations. Underwriting profits would emerge from the actual experience of companies using rates with a pro forma markup on sales, the underwriting profit provision. Investment profits would arise from the management of the portfolio of all invested assets. Since total profits from investment and underwriting were at least subject to ex-post review, they would be presumed to be reasonable overall for ratemaking purposes.[3] The underwriting profit provision used in ratemaking would then be deemed reasonable by implication. According to the industry, the process would satisfy the common statutory principle for regulatory review that "due consideration be given to . . . a reasonable margin for underwriting profit and contingencies." The Massachusetts ratemaking statute (c. 90, §113B and c. 152, §52C) somewhat similarly required that "due consideration shall be given to . . . a reasonable margin for underwriting profit and contingencies (and) investment income on unearned premium reserves and loss reserves. . . ."

Stone would not accept such an indirect treatment of underwriting and investment income. He saw no reason not to mesh the traditional insurance concept of *rate* regulation with the concept of *rate of return* regulation common in other regulated sectors of the U.S. economy.[4] The investment income question had just been considered in the well-known "New Jersey Remand Case," which held that New Jersey automobile insurance rates were to be computed to yield a 3.5 percent return on premiums including after-tax investment income from policyholder-supplied funds (Mintel 1983, p. 189).

Stone approved the use of the 2.5 percent underwriting profit provision for workers' compensation rates in 1975 but made it clear that the ratemaking format should change to accommodate investment income. His decision stated:

> To compute the true profit one must count all net gains from the insurance transaction, underwriting and investment, and compare those gains with the capital at risk in the transaction. This is the most commonly accepted rate of return measure in the relevant economic literature. While a $2\frac{1}{2}$ percent underwriting margin is not necessarily unreasonable, it is only a guess at the proper figure until this sort of calculation is made. (Stone 1975, p. 19)

In order to pursue this approach, however, Stone had to deal with an important problem: namely, that the insurance commissioner had very little control over the investment operations of insurers and no control over capital market outcomes which provided the investment returns.

Stone announced that he had overcome this problem, which he characterized as "the Gordian Knot of measuring investment return in insurance." He noted the wide variation in investment results across companies and over time and concluded that actual investment policies should be ignored in favor of a simple investment policy for ratemaking purposes. He would use the concept, suggested earlier by Cooper (1974), of including income from investments in risk-free U.S. Treasury securities as a minimal attainable investment standard for making insurance rates under his total return criterion. Stone warned the industry to be prepared for his version of total return regulation for all future rate decisions.

Stone's 1976 Automobile Decision

The calculation of an appropriate underwriting profit provision for automobile insurance became an area of acute controversy in Massachusetts with the 1976 Bodily Injury Liability Coverage Rate Decision issued by Stone in November 1975.[5] Stone implemented the total return concept by "finding that level of underwriting profit allowance which, if earned along with minimum reasonable investment results, would produce for the average carrier a rate of return on capital equal to that achieved by a typical nonregulated firm of similar risk characteristics."[6] In other words, if he could set an overall target return in some fashion, the underwriting profit provision would simply be chosen to yield the difference between the total return target and the risk-free investment return.

For 1976 rates, Stone adopted the concept of requiring total return to be calculated separately for bodily injury liability and property damage coverages based upon a judgment of the overall risk of the "regulatory standard" company.[7] For the bodily injury liability decision, he used a recent average return for 850 of the largest U.S. corporations plus some upward adjustment to account for the increased riskiness of the insurance sector during inflationary times because of "slow-pay" losses.[8] In his property damage decision later that same year, Stone agreed with expert witnesses at the hearings who suggested that the Capital Asset Pricing Model (CAPM) could provide the necessary measure of risk for calculating the target rate of return. The theoretical and empirical underpinnings of the CAPM beta to be used, however, appeared to be weak. These two hearings produced underwriting profit provisions of −4 percent for bodily injury coverages and 5 percent for property damage coverages.

The insurers challenged Commissioner Stone's 1976 automobile rates in an appeal to the Supreme Judicial Court of Massachusetts. They contended that the Commissioner's methodology erred in its choice of total rate of return criteria and failed to produce estimates of investment income that were realistic, that is, achievable with sound investment strategies. One industry witness had balked at the notion of using high new-money rates, albeit risk-free, at a time when the companies had sizable holdings of long-term, low-interest bonds originally purchased in the 1950s and 1960s.

The court ruled against the industry and embraced Stone's variant of total return regulation saying, in part,

> Traditionally, the allowance for profit was 1 percent of the total premium for compulsory coverages and 5 percent of the total premium for other coverages. But these figures were likely to be a very misleading indication of the actual profit made by the insurer on a given line of insurance. Because the premium dollars are paid to the insurers early in the policy year and the payment of insurance claims stretches over several years, the cash flow produces funds that the insurer can invest. . . . This income from investment is not directly adverted to in formulating the profit allowance by the traditional method. (*Attorney General* v. *Commissioner of Insurance 1976*)[9]

Stone's model formula was ad hoc but simple and patterned after the calculation of accounting returns. He proposed that the following equation be satisfied prospectively using currently available data:[10]

$$r = (1 - t)[sp + r_f + sR(1 - p)] \tag{6.1}$$

where

r = the target (total) rate of return
s = the premium-to-capital ratio
t = the tax rate
r_f = the risk-free rate
R = a discount factor from cash flow
p = the underwriting profit provision

Stone's formula includes the major parameters necessary to solve for the underwriting profit provision as the balancing unknown. The parameters included a cash flow schedule; an investment rate; an overall federal tax rate; invested capital both as a base for the total rate of return and as a measure of the leverage of the cash flow from premiums; and a measure of total risk in the formulation of the target rate of return. Stone had made "crude" estimates of the model and parametric inputs. In its approval of his methods, the Court warned that this imprecision might not be acceptable in future rate cases (Mintel 1983, p. 191).

Stone's rate of return concept was codified in the 1976 law regulating the Massachusetts experiment with competitive rating for automobile insurance. The new statute (c. 175E) replaced "due consideration . . . of investment income on unearned premium reserves and loss reserves . . ." with "Consideration shall be given . . . to a reasonable rate of return on capital after provision for investment income. . . ." Stone expected all companies to conform explicitly to his new scientific ratemaking methods as they competed for business. It did not happen that way, however, and the competitive rating system fell after only one round of rate filings. Intense political pressure as a result of large rate increases in some Boston territories resulted in the suspension of the competitive rating law in 1977 after only a three-month trial.

The 1978–1980 Rates

After the abortive attempt at open competition, automobile rates again were set by the Commissioner of Insurance for January 1, 1978. In his *Opinion, Findings, and Decision on 1978 Automobile Insurance Rates*, Stone adopted the methodology proposed by William Fairley and filed by the State Rating Bureau (SRB).[11] Fairley's method employed the CAPM in an attempt to develop a consistent relationship between the assumptions of cash flow, investment, and capital structure, on the one hand, and the treatment of risk on the other. The SRB suggested and Stone agreed to underwriting profit provisions of −4 percent on bodily injury coverages and 2 percent on property damage coverages for 1978 rates.

The central principle of the CAPM is that risk is divisible into systematic (market-related and nondiversifiable) and unsystematic components but that a risk premium is due the investor only for systematic risk.[12] The CAPM rate of return equation is

$$r = r_f + \beta[E(r_m) - r_f] \tag{6.2}$$

where

r = the required rate of return for a given asset
r_f = the risk-free rate of return
r_m = the rate of return on the market portfolio of risky assets
β = a measure of the asset's systematic risk, which is defined as $\text{cov}(r,r_m)/\text{var}(r_m)$ where cov( ) denotes covariance and var( ) denotes variance. E( ) denotes expected value.

Fairley's methodology used principles derived from the CAPM to impute income to the regulated company.[13] The company's target return on equity was presumed to be the risk-free rate adjusted for the riskiness of investments and underwriting, the latter by an "underwriting beta" which had to be measured indirectly.[14] The CAPM also was used to estimate the investment income that companies should expect to earn. Like the New Jersey Remand Decision, the Fairley model provided a target insurance operating return rather than a target total return. Moreover, since the CAPM was used to estimate both expected total return on equity and expected investment return, the Fairley model's equilibrium underwriting profit margin did not depend on the risk of the company's investment portfolio. This margin is given by (Fairley's equation 11a):

$$p = -kr_f - k\beta_L[E(r_m) - r_f] + \left[\frac{t}{(1 - t)s}\right] r_f \qquad (6.3)$$

where

p = the underwriting profit margin
k = a measure of the availability of investable policyholder funds, which is roughly equal to the ratio of reserves to premiums
r_f = the risk-free rate
β_L = the underwriting profit beta for the line of insurance
$E(r_m) - r_f$ = the market risk premium
t = the overall effective federal tax rate
s = the premium-to-surplus ratio

In words, the underwriting profit margin reflects a credit for the investment income on policyholders' funds that is offset by an expected reward for the risk of underwriting and by an allowance for federal income taxes.

The use of this model, or slight variations, produced the following underwriting profit provisions for automobile insurance rates for the years shown:[15]

	Bodily Injury Liability	*Property Damage*	*All Auto*
1977 rates	−4%	+5%	+2.3%
1978 rates	−4%	+2%	+0.2%
1979 rates	−8%	0%	−2.4%
1980 rates	−13%	−2%	−5.3%

The 1980 Remand and 1981 Rates

The hearings on 1979 and 1980 automobile insurance rates permitted meaningful examination of the Fairley model and its variations. The Massachusetts Rating Bureau showed that these models contained estimation error, and imputed to the industry investment income that did not match the industry's actual investment income. For these reasons, the decision by Commissioner Michael J. Sabbagh on 1980 automobile rates was appealed and subsequently reversed by the Supreme Judicial Court.[16] After noting that "simplifying assumptions" may need to be used to estimate the investment income attributable to a particular line of insurance, the Court established two principles to guide the use of such assumptions. First, they must be realistic. The industry must be able to earn the imputed investment income with real-world investment portfolios and actual taxes. Second, the assumptions must be internally consistent. The projected rates of return must correspond to the postulated portfolios, yields, taxes, and risk factors.

During the remand hearing on 1980 rates that occurred simultaneously with the hearing on 1981 rates, the industry introduced a comprehensive critique of the CAPM that was developed by Fielitz (1980). This critique claimed that the imprecision shown by empirical results of the CAPM made it unsuitable for ratemaking. The Commissioner, however, accepted the SRB's recommendation that the "Fairley CAPM model," as then modified to reincorporate the regulatory standard company assumption, be used for both the 1980 remand decision and for setting 1981 rates. The resulting underwriting profit provisions were

	Bodily Injury Liability	*Property Damage*	*All Auto*
1980 rates	−13.0%	−2.0%	−5.3%
1980 remand	−10.3%	+1.9%	−1.8%
1981 rates	−10.2%	+1.7%	−1.9%

where the original 1980 provisions also are shown for comparison purposes. The principal difference between the original and remand decisions on 1980 rates was that in the remand decision, following the Court's admonition about consistency, the Commissioner rejected the use of a 20 percent overall effective federal income tax rate and reverted to the use of the statutory 46 percent tax rate for both underwriting and investment income. This treatment was consistent with the original regulatory standard company portfolio assumption. This change was upheld in a subsequent Supreme Court decision.[17]

The 1982 and 1983 Rates

Given the string of rate decisions from 1976 to 1981 that approved the use of new-money investment rates rather than embedded yields, the industry abandoned its advocacy of the latter procedure and had the Fairley model reviewed by Myers and Cohn (1981).[18] Concentrating on defects in the form of the Fairley model, these authors proposed that it be replaced by a general multiperiod net present-value (discounted cash flow) model. The Myers-Cohn model was presented on behalf of the industry and scrutinized in late 1981 at the hearings on 1982 automobile rates. Its use was approved by Commissioner Sabbagh for setting 1982 rates.

The Myers-Cohn model was intended to be simpler, more general, more flexible, and more accurate than the Fairley models. The basic premise underlying this model is that the fair premium should equal the expected value of losses; expenses; federal income taxes on underwriting income—each discounted at a risk-adjusted rate; and federal income taxes on investment income—discounted at the risk-free rate. Premiums calculated in this way are intended to preserve the equity invested in the company and to give the investor a fair reward for the risk of underwriting. Algebraically, the model can be expressed as

$$\begin{aligned} PV(\text{premiums}) = {} & PV(\text{losses and expenses}) + \\ & PV(\text{federal income tax on investments}) + \\ & PV(\text{federal income tax on underwriting}) \end{aligned} \tag{6.4}$$

where $PV(\ )$ denotes present value.

The discount factor applicable to losses and expenses reflects investment income on the cash flow at current risk-free rates. Thus, the Myers-Cohn model is consistent with prior models that included investment income at a risk-free rate of return. The company and its stockholders are assumed to bear the risk and receive the reward for any risky investment strategy. The discount factor applicable to losses and expenses also reflects a risk adjustment that is chosen to yield a reasonable compensation for uncertainty in both the estimates of losses and expenses and in their realization—i.e., for the risk of underwriting. The fair premium is then calculated by including the present value of the federal income taxes on investment and underwriting income. This step requires the use of some method of allocating surplus to each line. The Myers-Cohn paper suggests allocating the surplus roughly in proportion to total outstanding reserves.[19]

In the Massachusetts applications of the Myers-Cohn model to date, the risk adjustment has been based on the CAPM; but, unlike the Fairley models, the Myers-Cohn model does not dictate the use of the CAPM or any other specific model of risk. The 1982 automobile decision set the profit provisions at −12.8 percent for bodily injury liability and 2.4 percent for property damage coverages, using a CAPM estimated beta for underwriting liabilities of −0.16. The underwriting profit provision for the combined coverages was −2.2 percent.

The decision on 1983 rates by Commissioner Sabbagh continued the use of the general format of the Myers-Cohn model. For 1982 rates, Sabbagh did not depart from the accounting notion of the strict proportionality of surplus to premiums, but he adopted all of the other Myers-Cohn recommendations including their assumption of a risk-free investment portfolio to estimate the federal tax burden. For 1983 rates, Sabbagh altered another aspect of the Myers-Cohn analysis and incorporated a recommendation from the Attorney General, originally suggested by Hill and Modigliani (1981), that the tax on investment income be derived from actual company portfolio holdings rather than the marginal corporate rate used by Myers and Cohn. Sabbagh's decision to replace the corporate tax rate of 46 percent on both investment income and underwriting income with a 28 percent rate on investment income and a 46 percent rate for underwriting losses substantially lowered the overall margins. The 1983 underwriting profit provisions were set at −22.3 percent for bodily injury liability and −1 percent for property damage coverages, resulting in an estimated overall margin of about −7.4 percent of premiums.

The industry appealed Sabbagh's decision on 1983 rates as having little or no support in the hearing record. The Court, relying on the principle of deference to the Commissioner, upheld the change in tax rates. It cited the Commissioner's use of a "new internal factor"—the alleged recognition for the first time of the impact of tax credits from underwriting losses—to support his reduction in the effective tax rate. In fact, there was no new factor, internal or otherwise. The Court actually had embraced an argument put forth by the Commissioner's appellate counsel that was absent from the hearing record and was not supported in the testimony of any expert witness. All models that properly account for taxes automatically turn underwriting tax liabilities into tax credits when underwriting profits become underwriting losses. The "internal factor" had been present in Stone's original model, the Fairley model, and the Myers-Cohn model.

Workers' Compensation Rates

The 1975–1978 Rates

Workers' compensation rate changes occur when the industry rating bureau files for a rate change and the Commissioner approves it. Changes in rates were generally made annually until Stone's decision in 1975. Thereafter, the increased level of contentiousness, along with the annual ratemaking developments in the Massachusetts automobile line, led to more intermittent filings and long delays in approvals.

Deteriorating country-wide underwriting results for workers' compensation in the mid-1970s and persistent high inflation led to a fundamental change in accepted ratemaking techniques. The National Council on Compensation Insurance (NCCI), the industry representative in thirty-nine states, began to put workers' compensation ratemaking on a prospective basis with the introduction of a loss-ratio trend method in its 1976 filings. This change was necessary in view of large increases in benefit costs arising from both legislation and inflation.

On July 13, 1977, the industry filed for a 31 percent increase in workers' compensation rates in Massachusetts. The industry argued that a reasonable return, considering past results, would be achieved with a 3.5 percent underwriting profit loading. This provision and other ratemaking concepts designed to adapt the NCCI trend methods to the Massachusetts environment drew stiff opposition from intervenors, leading Deputy Commissioner Andrew Giffin to deny the requested rate increase. Giffin relied upon objections raised by the SRB in its advisory filing.[20] In this filing, Fairley applied his model using cash flow patterns for workers' compensation and recommended an underwriting profit provision of −4.9 percent on behalf of the SRB.

Given that Massachusetts underwriting results had been deteriorating and that the last general rate change had occurred nearly three years earlier, the industry entered into a negotiated agreement for a rate increase of 9 percent effective April 1, 1978. The rate change included a change from 3.5 percent to the SRB recommended −4.9 percent provision for underwriting profit.[21]

The January 1, 1980 Rates

The January 1, 1980 general revision of rates was based primarily on a filing made by the industry bureau on June 14, 1979. Major revisions were proposed for the expense program, and a change to an unlimited payroll base was recommended. The industry filed without comment, and the SRB agreed to continue, the −4.9 percent underwriting profit provision in order to narrow the number of issues considered at the resultant hearing. In effect, the profit provision was still based upon the 1978 CAPM—Regulatory Standard Company theory and calculations.

The Filing for October 1, 1981 Rates

In September 1981, the industry bureau filed for a 30 percent rate revision to be effective October 1, 1981. The filing included a new method for the incorporation of trend in the rate-setting process and proposed the Myers-Cohn model as a means of incorporating investment income into the rates. Using the then current risk-free rate of 13.32 percent, new premium and loss cash flow estimates, a higher estimate of riskiness (beta) for the workers' compensation line, and allocation of surplus on a nearly one-to-one basis with premiums, the Myers-Cohn model recommended an underwriting profit provision of −1 percent. This figure was within the range of reasonable choices from −3.95 percent to 0.095 percent that varied according to the particular beta chosen.

Hearings on the 1981 filing were the longest on record. Thirty-seven hearing days were consumed throughout mid-1982. Each topic was discussed in minute detail. Since the Commissioner had used the new Myers-Cohn model to determine 1982 automobile rates, its acceptability was no longer a real issue. The input parameters to the model became the principal issues. The SRB opposed the use of the loss cash flow estimates, the allocation of surplus in the Myers-Cohn model, and the industry bureau's estimate of the workers' compensation underwriting beta.

A decision by Deputy Commissioner Mary Kingston on October 15, 1982 approved the incorporation of trend, finally putting Massachusetts on a prospective ratemaking track, but disapproved many of the profit parameters. The industry refiled for a 16 percent increase in rates using the SRB-recommended −12 percent underwriting profit provision. These rates became effective on January 1, 1983, three years after the previous general rate change. (These rates continue in use as of this writing.) The 11 percent difference between the original industry profit provision of −1 percent and the SRB provision of −12 percent clearly indicates the importance of the parametric inputs to the rate-setting process, regardless of the general theory and form of the model.

Key Issues and Parameters

One might ask why any of the models described in this chapter are necessary to determine premiums. The possibility exists that if the regulatory environment allowed for competitive rates, competition among insurers would produce fair premiums. If so, the output of financial models might simply provide insight into the level of market-determined rates. The regulatory process for Massachusetts automobile and workers' compensation insurance is, however, precisely the opposite of a competitive environment. The carriers are treated for ratemaking purposes as though they were a single company, a monopoly. Thus, a single premium must be determined that is fair to both policyholders and companies. Financial models, if used cautiously and with full knowledge of their limitations, can provide significant guidance in estimating fair premiums in this kind of environment.[22]

Experience with the profit models in Massachusetts since 1975 indicates several key estimation issues that must be confronted before the application of any model can produce reasonable results. This section of the chapter considers the estimation of (1) investment yields and tax rates, (2) the adjustment for the risk of underwriting, (3) the amount of surplus to allocate to a line, and (4) losses and expenses within the context of the current Myers-Cohn model.[23]

Investment Yield and Taxes

The use of risk-free yields for imputing investment returns obviously requires the selection of appropriate yields on risk-free securities. Ideally, risk-free yields available during the time period in which the surplus is committed and the policy cash flow, which may extend over several years, is invested are the most appropriate to use. U.S. Treasury yields are customarily used as proxies for taxable risk-free one-period investment yields. Unfortunately, there seems to be no acceptable method available for projecting future Treasury yields. At various times, recommendations have been made in the Massachusetts hearings to obtain estimates from the Treasury futures markets or to use forward rates inherent in the term structure of Treasury yields or even to use the latest day's yield rates. Although each method had some theoretical appeal, all were found to lack the stability necessary for ratemaking.

The practical solution underlying most of the rate decisions was to use an average of the most recent twelve months of yields for all Treasury securities. This procedure has the advantage of being simple and based upon indisputable data. The twelve-month choice lessens fluctuations through the averaging process while reflecting substantial changes from year to year. All variations in economic conditions that occur over time are thus captured and reflected in the rates. In addition, the consistent use of the twelve-month averages precludes selectivity bias by parties involved in the ratemaking process, an important consideration in Massachusetts. The risk-free rates used in actual rate decisions in Massachusetts from 1978 to 1983 and the Treasury yields actually experienced during those years are as follows:

	Risk-Free Rate	*Actual Treasury Yield*
1978	6.20	8.34
1979	8.19	10.67
1980	12.24	12.05
1981	11.43	14.78
1982	14.75	12.27
1983	14.01	9.57
Six-year average	11.14	11.28

As would be expected, interest rate movements often produced sizable differences between the decision rates and actual yield rates in individual years. However, the average difference for the entire period was small.

Since policyholders are to be credited with after-tax investment income, an estimate of the effective federal income tax rate is also necessary. Prior to 1981, little, if any, attention was paid in the literature to the large and crucial role that federal income taxes would play in the ratemaking models. Indeed, Fairley (1979, p. 202) remarked that "the introduction of corporate taxes modifies the solution ... by adding to it a term depending upon the tax rate t and the premium to capital ratio s ... the added term is not, however, quantitatively very important." However, this is not the case, as was illustrated by the previous discussion of Massachusetts automobile rates before and after the 1980 remand decision.

The early Massachusetts profit models allowed for federal income taxes by using one tax rate for both investment and underwriting income. Modifications to the Fairley model prepared by Hill and Modigliani (1981) allowed for underwriting and investment income to be treated separately for tax purposes. This procedure is more consistent with the treatment of taxes for insurance companies in the U.S. Tax Code. It does, however, produce more dramatic differences by line, principally because of the effect of underwriting tax credits on lines with negative underwriting margins.

As the 1983 automobile insurance decision demonstrates, the choice of the effective investment tax rate, not the overall tax rate, is now the relevant issue.[24] The overall profit margins based on the proposed use of a 46 percent investment tax rate and the 28 percent investment tax rate that was adopted in the decision differed by 5.2 percent, as can be seen in the following 1983 tabulation.

	Investment Tax Rate	*Underwriting Tax Rate*	*Overall (All-Auto) Profit Margin*
Proposed	46%	46%	−2.2%
Adopted	28%	46%	−7.4%

The key question concerning the treatment of taxes is how to estimate the effective investment tax rate from the same market data that are being used to estimate risk-free yields. Answering this question presents both theoretical and empirical difficulties. From a theoretical standpoint, it is the present value of income taxes that must be estimated. Thus, the estimate should consider the complex mixture of risk, taxes, and yields in insurance company asset portfolios. Myers and Cohn (1981) alluded to this complexity by stating that "these are current matters of great controversy in financial economics." Their use of the marginal corporate tax rate of 46 percent was, as Myers characterized it, "a good first approximation." More recently, Myers has shown that the present value of the investment tax liability arising from *any* investment portfolio depends only on the risk-free rate and the effective tax rate for the portfolio.[25] Of course, the problem of finding the effective tax rate for use in the regulatory model remains.

On the empirical side, one must be able to get consistent and reliable estimates of the magnitudes of the risk adjustments and tax effects in security prices. Before moving away from the 46 percent investment tax rate, one must be prepared to demonstrate the existence of a portfolio that yields higher returns after adjusting for both risk and taxes than would a portfolio composed of taxable risk-free securities. One such portfolio was considered recently in the industry filing for 1985 rates. While details are provided elsewhere (Derrig 1985), the important empirical finding was that a portfolio of tax-exempt securities in 1984, immunized to the automobile policy cash flows, showed an effective tax rate of about 43 percent after adjusting for risk.[26] Thus, this analysis suggests that an appropriate after-tax new-money rate to use to impute investment income on policyholder funds for the automobile line would be 57 percent of the current Treasury yields matched to the policy cash flows.[27] Further research is needed to clarify this question and produce consistent theoretical and empirical results.

Reward for the Risk of Underwriting

All of the ratemaking models considered here attempt to price the insurance transaction. The insured transfers the risk of an uncertain economic loss to the insurer by paying the premium. If the premium is fair, it will be just sufficient to cover expected costs and provide an expected profit (return to capital) commensurate with the risk borne by the insurer. Without some expected profit, the insurer has no incentive to commit capital to support the insurance contract.

Each of the Massachusetts models had some component designed to compensate the insurer for risk bearing. Each method of reflecting the insurer's risk brought unique problems of measurement. Stone's model attempted to provide an appropriate target return for overall company operations, both underwriting and investment. Fairley's models included an expected risk-loading in the underwriting margin based on the CAPM. The Myers-Cohn model used a risk-adjusted discount rate for losses and expenses. Discounting losses and expenses at a rate lower than the risk-free rate raises the fair premium in accordance with the size of the risk adjustment.

The Massachusetts implementations of the Myers-Cohn model have used an estimated risk adjustment based on the CAPM, but this general net present-value model would allow for any method of estimating risk. Most recently, the risk adjustment assumed a beta for underwriting liabilities of -0.16 and a market risk premium of 9 percent. The latter figure also was used by Hill and Modigliani (1981). The use of these values reduces the risk-free component of the discount rate by 1.44 percent (0.16×0.09).

The relationship between particular estimates of unobservable underwriting betas or of risk-adjusted discount rates and more widely used measures of financial performance is of interest. Stone's model had the advantage of stating the risk adjustment in terms of an overall rate of return which in turn could be compared to all-industry rates of return to provide some guidance as to its reasonableness. One method for assessing the magnitude of the risk adjustment in the Myers-Cohn model is to determine the percentage of the fair premium that is designed to compensate for risk.

The basic idea underlying this method is that the premium calculated using risk-free discount rates in this model would contain no reward for risk. A comparison of this premium with the fair premium—i.e., that calculated using a risk-adjusted discount rate—then can be used to obtain the expected reward for risk as a percentage of the fair premium. For instance, the five-quarter example presented in the appendix to the Myers-Cohn paper yields a fair premium of $99.28 per $100 of losses. Replacing the risk-adjusted value of losses (0.9653) and taxes (0.1931) by the risk-free value of losses (0.9558) and taxes (0.1912) gives a risk-free premium of $98.30 per $100 of losses. Thus, $0.98 ($99.28 − $98.30) is being added to the riskless premium to account for the risk of underwriting in this simple example. This amounts to about 1 percent of the fair premium.[28]

In the October 1, 1981 workers' compensation filing, the risk-loading was calculated for various values of the underwriting beta. Those results showed that, given all the other parameters, there was a 1 percent risk-loading in the fair premium for each −0.1 of the underwriting liability beta: for example, a beta of −0.16 gave a risk-loading of 1.6 percent of premium. The recommended profit margin of −1 percent included a risk-loading of about 4 percent of premium. This compared favorably with the operating profit after all federal income taxes of 5.75 percent for 1976–1980 and 3.92 percent for 1971–1980 derived from a Best's study of total returns for companies operating in Texas (Callaghan and Derrig 1982b, pp. 46–47, 59).

The issue of the proper risk-loading clearly is one of measurement. The indirect methods of Fairley, Hill and Modigliani, and others produce results that are internally consistent, but they are subject to serious problems arising either from a lack of data or from the inherent imprecision in empirical estimates of CAPM betas. It may also be the case, as Callaghan and Derrig (1982b) contend, that insurance company risk is undervalued using the CAPM beta as a measure of risk. Indeed, Turner (1981) demonstrates that the presence of nonmarket risks produces systematic deviations in equilibrium prices from those predicted by the CAPM.[29] The above method of viewing the risk-loading as a percentage of premium allows the values to be checked for reasonableness against long-term industry averages until more suitable methods of estimating the risk-loading are developed.

The Allocation of Surplus

Another area of continual dispute in the application of the profit models has been the amount of surplus needed to support each line of insurance. The allocation of the proper amount of surplus is important because, as Myers and Cohn (1981) showed, the fair premium must include the present value of the taxes on the investment income attributable to the surplus supporting the policy. As more or less surplus is allocated to the line of insurance, higher or lower tax burdens will be inferred with resultant higher or lower premiums and underwriting profit margins.

Conventional accounting wisdom and the early Stone-Fairley models related surplus needs to premiums. The so-called "Kenney Rule" was used by Stone in 1976 to estimate surplus needs at one-half of premium volume. Although this seemed like the proper course to take for overall regulatory purposes, the economics-based cash flow methodologies required an allocation of surplus to each line of insurance.

During the hearing on the 1981 workers' compensation rates, it was shown that Fairley's treatment of surplus would not produce equal rates of return for equally risky amounts of surplus committed over the same period of time (Callaghan and Derrig 1982a). Fairley's model would yield equal rates of return for equally risky commitments of surplus only if the variable ks, roughly the ratio of total reserves to surplus, were held constant. This implied that the overall surplus level should be related to reserves, not premiums, and that the allocation by line should also be by reserves rather than premiums.

For simplicity, these points can be illustrated using the simple no-tax version of the Fairley model. Using Fairley's estimates of k (reserves-to-premiums ratio) for automobile and workers' compensation insurance (Fairley 1979, p. 197) and assuming a constant premium-to-surplus ratio by line, the following target rates of return on equity for each line would be obtained using the model without income taxes:[30]

	Reserves-to-Premiums	*Premiums-to-Surplus*	*Return on Equity*
Auto BI	1.60	2	30.00%
Auto PD	0.31	2	13.88%
Workers' Comp.	1.60	2	30.00%

Alternatively, allocating surplus proportional to k for each line (so that the by-line premium-to-surplus ratio becomes $2/k$) yields the following:

	Reserves-to-Premiums	*Premiums-to-Surplus*	*Return on Equity*
Auto BI	1.60	1.25	22.50%
Auto PD	0.31	6.45	22.50%
Workers' Comp.	1.60	1.25	22.50%

The conclusion of this analysis was that there had to be a per-period relationship between the amount of surplus allocated to a line and the relative magnitude of the risk for a line. Furthermore, if the per-period risk adjustment was to be constant for each period and line, as in all applications to date in Massachusetts, then the allocation of surplus each period would need to be in proportion to outstanding reserves for each line. Thus, it followed that more surplus should be committed to the long-tailed, large-reserve, Schedule P lines than to the short-term, small-reserve, Schedule O lines of insurance. Recent results show that premium-to-surplus ratios corresponding to this method of allocation would be about one for automobile bodily injury and workers' compensation, two for automobile property damage liability, and three for automobile physical damage.

The multiperiod Myers-Cohn model explicitly models the flow of surplus based on the assumption that companies hold surplus for a longer period of time on long-tailed lines. Since surplus is exposed to underwriting risk for a longer period of time, companies require more cumulative compensation on long-tailed lines—just as in the Fairley model—but the per-period rate of return on surplus is constant among lines when the per-period measure of risk is assumed to be constant.

The issue of the proper allocation of surplus by line stands unresolved at this time. Support for allocating surplus in proportion to reserves, rather than to premiums, was expressed in the recent report by the NAIC Task Force on Investment Income (*Report of the Task Force* 1984, p. 46), which stated that "allocation on the basis of liabilities would appear to be more sound from a theoretical standpoint." However, this view has yet to be adopted in Massachusetts.

The Estimates of Losses and Expenses

A basic principle upon which any ex-ante profit model should be based is that the expected profits are, in fact, attainable. Stated differently, these methodologies assume that the rest of the rating procedure will produce unbiased results so that actual profits will be randomly distributed around the expected value. Fairley observed that realized insurance industry underwriting profits were seven to eight percentage points less than rate provision profit targets. He conjectured that the industry had not earned excessive profits on average, despite the failure of ratemaking methods to explicitly reflect investment income, and that the shortfall was due to competitive and regulatory market pressures that caused losses and expenses to be persistently underestimated in the rates. The NAIC Investment Income Task Force also noted (p. 25): "If the estimate of losses and expenses is a priori biased one way or another, the method used to estimate losses and expenses should be changed to remove that bias." Any move to set profit margins according to financial models, therefore, demands unbiased forecasts of losses and expenses to produce meaningful results, and also leaves little room for error in the absence of a contingency loading.

Recent Massachusetts results for automobile and workers' compensation insurance suggest that whatever the theory may demand, external pressures may produce biased estimates of expected losses and expenses. As reported elsewhere in detail (Derrig 1984), and illustrated in the next section, the approved Massachusetts automobile and workers' compensation rates have consistently underestimated losses and expenses.

Before briefly reviewing these results, it is worth emphasizing why precision in estimating losses and expenses is necessary. First, as stated before, all the financial models require a precise estimate of losses and expenses. Otherwise, the target profit levels are illusory. Second, when these models are used ex-ante, there is usually no legal possibility of recoupment of operating losses if losses and expenses are systematically underestimated. Third, it was noted in the previous section that the reward for underwriting risk is a relatively small percentage of premiums. As a result, even a small underestimate of losses and expenses (e.g., 2–4 percent) is enough to wipe out the entire risk-loading. Finally, as presently structured, the financial models do not contain any feedback mechanism, contingency factor, or catastrophe provision. The absence of these traditional devices for assuring long-run profits puts a heavy burden on the precision of the financial models, a burden that may well exceed the current state of knowledge.

Table 6-1. Effects of Parameter Inputs on the Underwriting Profit Provision for the Myers-Cohn Model

Underwriting Risk	*Investment Yield/Tax Rate*					
	6%/28%	*6%/46%*	*10%/28%*	*10%/46%*	*14%/28%*	*14%/46%*
1. Block Surplus						
Beta = 0	−10.4%	−6.3%	−17.7%	−10.5%	−25.4%	−14.9%
Beta = −0.16	−6.2	−2.2	−13.4	−6.5	−20.9	−10.8
Beta = −0.33	−1.8	+2.1	−8.9	−2.2	−16.3	−6.6
Beta = −0.50	+2.5	+6.2	−4.5	+1.9	−11.8	−2.5
2. Flow Surplus						
Beta = 0	−9.2%	−4.3%	−15.8%	−7.3%	−22.6%	−10.4%
Beta = −0.16	−5.0	−0.3	−11.5	−3.3	−18.3	−6.5
Beta = −0.33	−0.7	+3.9	−7.1	+0.8	−13.8	−2.4
Beta = −0.50	+3.6	+7.9	−2.7	+4.8	−9.4	+1.5

Note: Underlying cash flows approximate the automobile bodily injury flows in Massachusetts. The underwriting tax rate is always 46 percent, the underwriting tax flow is assumed to occur quarterly during year one. Surplus is chosen proportional (2 to 1) to premiums during year one (Block) or to outstanding liabilities per quarter (Flow).

Sensitivity of Profit Provisions and Review of Results

Table 6-1 illustrates the sensitivity of the underwriting profit provisions to the choice of input parameters for a long-tailed line of insurance using the Myers-Cohn model.[31] The choice of an investment tax rate gives rise to 6–8 percent differences in the underwriting profit provision, even for a moderate risk-free yield (10 percent). Similarly, there is a difference of about 2 percent in the profit provision for each 0.1 change in the beta. Finally, the allocation method for surplus (*block* for allocation with premiums, *flow* for allocation with reserves) produces a 2–4 percent difference in outcomes. One can see by reviewing the table that these parametric choices have compounding effects as well.

While the immediate concern in the early Massachusetts models was to estimate the investment yield rate, the sensitivity of the profit provisions illustrated by table 6-1 demonstrates the need either to find better estimation techniques or to exercise extreme caution in applying the results. For example, the profit provisions for automobile bodily injury range from −17.7 to 4.8 percent, even when the risk-free interest rate is fixed at 10 percent. The magnitude of this range would seem to dwarf a 2 percent risk-loading.

Table 6-2 reports the target underwriting profit provisions set annually by the Commissioner for the automobile line and underlying the rates approved by the Commissioner for workers' compensation for the latest six policy years with available data. These targets are compared with the best current estimate of the actual underwriting profits. The automobile data cover the policy year 1978, the first year after competitive rating, through 1983. The workers' compensation data are for 1976–1981, the latest for which reasonably mature data are available. As can be seen, actual results fell short of the targets by about 6 percent of premiums for automobile insurance and by about 11 percent of premiums for workers' compensation.[32]

The question arises as to why this persistent shortfall has occurred. First it is worth noting that the shortfalls between manual rate underwriting profit provisions and realized underwriting profits that were noted by Fairley (1979) also have occurred countrywide in recent years (e.g., Haayen 1983). The presumption by Fairley was that the country-wide shortfalls were due to the implicit inclusion of investment income in the determination of premiums. The expectation was that if investment income could be handled in a formal analytic manner, such shortfalls would not occur. However, a persistent shortfall has occurred in Massachusetts despite the advent of "scientific ratemaking" and the inclusion of investment income in manual rates.

Table 6-2. Comparison of Target Underwriting Profit with Actual Underwriting Results

	Automobile				*Workers' Compensation*		
Policy Year	*Target Underwriting Profit*	*Actual Underwriting Profit*	*Actual Minus Target*	*Policy Year*	*Target Underwriting Profit*	*Actual Underwriting Profit*	*Actual Minus Target*
1978	+0.2%	−2.5%	−2.7%	1976	+2.5%	−10.1%	−12.6%
1979	−2.5	−13.7	−11.2	1977	+2.5	−8.6	−11.1
1980	−1.9	−9.6	−7.7	1978	−3.1	−19.1	−16.0
1981	−2.0	−12.9	−10.9	1979	−4.9	−19.5	−14.6
1982	−2.3	−7.5	−5.2	1980	−4.9	−7.6	−2.7
1983	−7.7	−6.3	+1.4	1981	−4.9	−11.6	−6.7
Six-year average	−2.7%	−8.8%	−6.1%	Six-year average	−2.1%	−12.7%	−10.6%

Note: Automobile actual underwriting profit results are for major coverages only with losses developed to 60 months. Targets may differ from the All-Auto provision in the text due to the use of actual premium weights by coverage. The 1980 target is from the remand decision. Workers' compensation underwriting profit results are estimated using developed losses as of December 31, 1983. No dividends are considered and standard earned premium is used as a base.

Source: Massachusetts Rating Bureau.

The shortfalls in Massachusetts automobile and workers' compensation have not resulted from the inclusion of investment income in ratemaking. They instead reflect the use of inadequate estimates of losses and expenses. The regulatory authorities, especially in 1978 and 1979, quickly embraced the downward influence on rates due to the inclusion of investment income. At the same time, they resisted efforts to accurately estimate loss and expense costs. Hindsight suggests that the Insurance Department's refusal to accept the prospective trend methodology for workers' compensation during the period 1977–1982 may have been responsible for the mismatch of target and realized results. For automobile insurance, the explanation may be similar. Average underestimates in predicted loss costs of more than 8 percent per coverage per year led directly to the poor results for 1978–83, although some improvements occurred in the last two years of this period. The results shown in table 6-2 indicate how fragile a risk-loading of only 2 percent of premiums ($\beta = -0.16$) really is, especially when viewed in conjunction with the sensitivity of target profit provisions to variation in the input parameters that is illustrated in table 6-1.

The major problem of accurately estimating losses and expenses is not insurmountable if regulators are willing to accept bad news when it comes in the form of higher costs. The underwriting comparison for 1982 and 1983 in Massachusetts automobile insurance shows that reasonably accurate estimates can be made.[33] Likewise, the improved results for workers' compensation in 1980 and 1981 most likely stemmed from the approval of the change to an unlimited payroll exposure base, a change that was tantamount to a partial acceptance of a trending methodology.

Conclusion

This paper has reviewed the Massachusetts experiment with including investment income in ratemaking from 1976 to 1983. The use of financial models has shown a clear progression from Commissioner Stone's one-period accounting model in 1976 to the more general multiperiod net present-value model of Myers and Cohn in 1981. The importance of the parametric inputs to the models has been illustrated. Questions about the appropriate measures of risk, allocation of surplus, and effective tax rates on investments provide challenges for future research. However, review of underwriting results clearly indicates that elegant theory and accurate parameter estimation will mean nothing if the basic ratemaking problem of estimating losses and expenses is handled unfairly or with poorly performing methods. On the other hand, if the issue of loss and expense estimation can be dealt with fairly, improved methods of applying financial models may produce satisfactory results.

It also should be evident that the use of economic valuation models, such as the fair-premium model of Myers and Cohn or even the more sophisticated model by Kraus and Ross (1982), requires a different mindset. The majority of insurance company observers view the industry in terms of accounting data and results. Economic and accounting values should be reconcilable over time, but the task, as evidenced by the surplus allocation issue, may not be easy. Harder still is the proper role that actual company investment portfolio results should play in this complex economic analysis. Stone said that he had cut the "Gordian Knot," but it was cut only by decree, not by natural causes. There may yet be a fundamental role for actual portfolio performance in the ratemaking process.

The alleged purpose of the use of these financial models by regulators is to produce results that would occur in a competitive market. In states that do not regulate rates, the competitive market probably does a decent job of allocating costs and producing fair profits. In these cases, fair-premium models may be useful for evaluation purposes. They may provide guidance in pricing at the company level, or they may provide benchmarks for assessing underwriting results. If, however, ex-ante financial models of the variety found in Massachusetts are to be used in rate regulation, participants should be prepared for seemingly endless haggling over disputed methods and parameters.[34]

Notes

1. Stone served as Commissioner of Insurance in Massachusetts from 1975–1979. His academic background in economics, finance, and insurance qualified him to consider the investment income issue.

2. Methods that were proposed but not approved will not be discussed. These include methods based upon actual company portfolio results, the so-called embedded-yield accounting approach, developed by the author and others, and the State Rating Bureau discounted cash flow model developed by Stefan Peters and Howard C. Mahler.

3. For example, the National Association of Insurance Commissioners (NAIC) publishes combined underwriting and investment income results annually in the *NAIC Report on Profitability by Line and State*. See also the thirty-year (1950–1980) review by an Advisory Committee to the NAIC (Haayen 1983).

4. As Mintel points out (1983, p. 87), the notion of using rate of return on capital in setting insurance rates goes back at least to an automobile rate case brought by the city of Philadelphia in 1961.

5. Underwriting profit provisions for commercial automobile insurance were set equal to those in the state-made rates for private passenger automobile insurance until 1981 when a system of limited competitive rating was introduced in Massachusetts. References to

automobile insurance in the text will refer to both lines through 1981 and private passenger only subsequent to 1981.

6. This concept, as contained in his 1976 automobile rate decision (p. 25), was designed to conform with the criterion in the landmark utility regulation case, *Federal Power Commission* v. *Hope Natural Gas Company*, 320 U.S. 591 (1944).

7. In Massachusetts, property damage coverages include both property damage liability and physical damage coverages (collision and comprehensive).

8. The target return for bodily injury liability coverages had a judgmentally added 1.5 percent to guard against "inflation risk" and "unforeseen economic contingencies." Stone's original target rates of return were based upon returns earned by other comparable nonregulated companies on their total capital rather than their equity capital. The use of total capital was criticized in the Massachusetts Supreme Judicial Court's 1976 decision discussed below.

9. *Attorney General* v. *Commissioner of Insurance*, 353 N.E. 2d 745, 370 Mass. 791 (1976). The Supreme Judicial Court decision was a single decision written for five consolidated cases, three by the industry and two by the Attorney General. See also Mintel (1983, p. 190).

10. Equation (6.1) was used by Stone in his prescribed filing form for competitive rating in 1977. No formal equation was set forth in the 1976 decisions.

11. The SRB was created in 1976 by the Massachusetts Legislature at Stone's request in order to provide additional actuarial expertise to the Division of Insurance and to monitor the competitive rating system. The SRB made a complete filing for 1978 and subsequent rates, usually in opposition to the industry proposal.

12. For background on the CAPM, see, for example, Brealey and Myers (1981, pp. 142–152).

13. For a more extensive explanation of this methodology, see Fairley (1979), which is reprinted as chapter 1 of this volume.

14. Security betas commonly are measured by regressing the observed rate of return of the security on the rate of return on a market proxy. Because an underwriting security does not trade in an open market, the beta of underwriting must be measured in a different fashion. See, for example, Hill and Modigliani (1981), a revised version of which is included as chapter 2 of this volume, and Cummins and Harrington (1985).

15. The provision for *All Auto*, i.e., for both coverages combined, is estimated by weighting the bodily injury liability provision by 30 percent and the property damage provision by 70 percent. These percentages approximate the actual percentages of total earned premiums accounted for by the lines for this period. The 1977 figures are those suggested by the Division of Insurance of competitive rates.

16. *Massachusetts Automobile and Accident Prevention Bureau* v. *Commissioner of Insurance*, 411 N.E. 2d 762, 381 Mass 592 (1980). See also Mintel (1983, p. 191). Sabbagh served as Commissioner of Insurance from 1980–1984. A long-time member of the regulatory staff of the Division of Insurance, Sabbagh did not possess Stone's background in rate-making theory, but he was well versed in the practical aspects of the property-casualty insurance business.

17. *Massachusetts Automobile Rating and Accident Prevention Bureau* v. *Commissioner of Insurance*, 424 N.E. 2d 1127, 384 Mass 333 (1981).

18. A revised version of the Myers-Cohn paper is included as chapter 3 of this volume.

19. The choice of a surplus allocation procedure, which has been subject to controversy since 1975, is discussed further later in the paper.

20. Advisory Filing of State Rating Bureau, November 7, 1977. Section H dealt with rate

of return and the profit provision.

21. The approved filing also excluded all aspects of the prospective ratemaking changes recommended by the Industry Bureau.

22. The efficacy of competitive systems versus regulated systems of ratemaking is beyond the scope of this paper. See, for example, the general discussion of competition in workers' compensation by Appel (1985). Also see Harrington (1984).

23. While significant difficulty also can be encountered in estimating cash flow schedules, this problem, which primarily reflects data limitations, is not considered here.

24. Low actual tax rates have occurred recently, primarily because of the combined effects of large tax-exempt bond holdings and large tax credits generated by underwriting losses. Since the models automatically adjust the tax burden for underwriting losses, the remaining modeling issue is the effective tax rate on the investment portfolio.

25. See the Massachusetts Hearing on 1985 Private Passenger Automobile Rates, Exhibit 143.

26. Derrig (1985) also provides a more complete discussion of the income tax question in ratemaking.

27. Stone's original estimate for risk-free yields used Treasury securities whose maturities matched the loss and expense liabilities. The refined concept of duration-matched securities is more appropriate. See Derrig (1985) for further discussion.

28. This ratio can be estimated easily by the formula $1 - a/b$ where a equals the risk-free discounted value of losses and b equals the risk-adjusted discounted value of losses. This formula assumes that the underwriting tax liability is incurred as the losses are paid. The use of other assumptions will change the formula but the general approach will remain valid.

29. Details of the Turner (1981) study are presented elsewhere in this volume.

30. Details of these calculations are provided by Callaghan and Derrig (1982).

31. An appendix to Myers and Cohn (1981) shows similar results.

32. A more detailed review is provided by Derrig (1984).

33. For these years, refinements were accepted for claim cost trend methods and frequency models.

34. The recently concluded Massachusetts hearing on 1985 automobile insurance rates consumed a record 48 hearing days with 21 days devoted to underwriting profit provisions.

References

Appel, D. 1985. Regulating competition: The case of workers' compensation insurance. *Journal of Insurance Regulation* 3(June):409–425.

Brealey, R., and S. Myers. 1981. *Principles of Corporate Finance*. New York: McGraw-Hill.

Callaghan, A., Jr. and R. Derrig. 1982a. Position paper on surplus. Hearing on Massachusetts Workers' Compensation Rates, Exhibit 69, June.

Callaghan, A., Jr., and R. Derrig. 1982b. Position paper on the risk and reward for underwriting. Hearing on Massachusetts Workers' Compensation Rates, Exhibit 70, June.

Cooper, R. 1974. *Investment Return and Property-Liability Insurance Ratemaking*. Homewood, IL: Richard D. Irwin.

Cummins, J. D., and S. Harrington. 1985. Property-liability insurance rate regulation: Estimation of underwriting betas using quarterly profit data. *Journal of Risk and Insurance* 52(March):16–43.

Derrig, R. 1984. An aspect of pricing risk: Lessons from Massachusetts. *Economic Issues in Workers' Compensation Conference*. New York: National Council on Compensation Insurance.

Derrig, R. 1985. The effect of federal income taxes on investment income in property-liability ratemaking. Massachusetts Rating Bureaus.

Fairley, W. 1979. Investment income and profit margins in property-liability insurance: Theory and empirical results. *Bell Journal of Economics* 10(Spring): 192–210.

Fielitz, B. 1980. A critique of the CAPM in property-liability insurance rate setting decisions. *Advisory Filing of the Massachusetts Automobile and Accident Prevention Bureau for 1981 Rates*, August.

Haayen, R. 1983. *Report of the Advisory Committee to the NAIC Task Force on Profitability and Investment Income*. Northbrook, IL: Allstate Insurance Company.

Harrington, S. 1984. The impact of rate regulation on prices and underwriting results in the property-liability insurance industry: A survey. *Journal of Risk and Insurance* 51(December):577–623.

Hill, R., and F. Modigliani. 1981. The Massachusetts model of profit regulation in non-life insurance: An appraisal and extensions. Paper prepared for Massachusetts Automobile Insurance Rate Hearings, August.

Kraus, A., and S. Ross. 1982. The determinants of fair profits for the property-liability insurance firm. *Journal of Finance* 37(September):1015–1028.

Mintel, J. 1983. *Insurance Rate Litigation*. Boston, MA: Kluwer-Nijhoff.

Myers, S., and R. Cohn. 1981. Insurance rate of return regulation and the capital asset pricing model. *Advisory Filing of the Massachusetts Automobile and Accident Prevention Bureau for 1982 Rates*, August.

Report of the Investment Income Task Force to the National Association of Insurance Commissioners. 1984. Reprinted in *Journal of Insurance Regulation* 3(September):39–112 and (December):153–181.

Stone, J. 1975. *Opinion, Findings and Decision on 1975 Workmen's Compensation Rates*. Division of Insurance, Commonwealth of Massachusetts.

Turner, A. 1981. Insurance markets and the behavior of competitive insurance firms. Ph.D. Dissertation, University of Pennsylvania.

Index